# ESSENTIALS OF
# FORENSIC SCIENCE

# Firearms and
# Fingerprints

# ESSENTIALS OF
# FORENSIC SCIENCE

# Firearms and Fingerprints

Edward Hueske

SET EDITOR
Suzanne Bell, Ph.D.

☑ Facts On File
*An imprint of Infobase Publishing*

FIREARMS AND FINGERPRINTS

Copyright © 2009 by Edward Hueske

Facts On File, Inc.
An imprint of Infobase Publishing
132 West 31st Street
New York NY 10001

**Library of Congress Cataloging-in-Publication Data**

Hueske, Edward E.
    Firearms and fingerprints / Edward Hueske.
        p. cm. — (Essential of forensic science)
    Includes bibliographical references and index.
    ISBN-13: 978-0-8160-5512-8
    ISBN-10: 0-8160-5512-2
    1. Fingerprints—Identification. 2. Forensic ballistics. 3. Forensic sciences—Vocational guidance. 4. Criminal investigation—Vocational guidance. I. Title.
    HV6074.H84 2008
    363.2562—dc22   2008001720

Facts On File books are available at special discounts when purchased in bulk quantities for businesses, associations, institutions, or sales promotions. Please call our Special Sales Department in New York at (212) 967-8800 or (800) 322-8755.

You can find Facts On File on the World Wide Web at http://www.factsonfile.com

Text design by Erik Lindstrom
Illustrations by Accurate Art, Inc.

Printed in the United States of America

MP ML 10 9 8 7 6 5 4 3 2 1

This book is printed on acid-free paper and contains 30 percent post-consumer content.

*This book is dedicated to Gretchen, my precious wife of more than 40 years, who has stood by me through thick and thin, put up with my workaholic tendencies, and kept the home fires burning as I have gallivanted across the country lecturing and testifying.*

# CONTENTS

# PREFACE

**F**orensic science has become in the early 21st century what the space race was in the 1960s—an accessible and inspiring window into the world of science. The surge in popularity that began in the latter part of the 20th century echoes a boom that began in the later part of the 19th century and was labeled the "Sherlock Holmes effect." Today it is called the "C.S.I. effect," but the consequences are the same as they were a century ago. The public has developed a seemingly insatiable appetite for anything forensic, be it fiction, reality, or somewhere between.

Essentials of Forensic Science is a set that is written in response to this thirst for knowledge and information. Written by eminent forensic scientists, the books cover the critical core of forensic science from its earliest inception to the modern laboratory and courtroom.

Forensic science is broadly defined as the application of science to legal matters, be they criminal cases or civil lawsuits. The history of the law dates back to the earliest civilizations, such as the Sumerians and the Egyptians, starting around 5000 B.C.E. The roots of science are older than civilization. Early humans understood how to make tools, how to cook food, how to distinguish between edible and inedible plants, and how to make rudimentary paints. This knowledge was technical and not based on any underlying unifying principles. The core of these behaviors is the drive to learn, which as a survival strategy was invaluable. Humans learned to cope with different environments and conditions, allowing adaptation when other organisms could not. Ironically, the information encoded in human DNA gives us the ability to analyze, classify, and type it.

Science as a formalized system of thinking can be traced to the ancient Greeks, who were the first to impose systematic patterns of thought and analysis to observations. This occurred around 500 B.C.E. The Greeks organized ideas about the natural world and were able to conceive of advanced concepts. They postulated the atom (from the Greek word *atomos*) as the fundamental unit of all matter. The Greeks were also among the first to study anatomy, medicine, and physiology in a systematic way and to leave extensive written records of their work. They also formalized the concept of the autopsy.

From ancient roots to modern practice the history of forensic science winds through the Middle Ages, alchemy, and the fear of poisoning. In 1840 pivotal scientific testimony was given by Mathieu-Joseph-Bonaventure (Mateu Josep Bonaventura) Orfila (1787–1853) in a trial in Paris related to a suspected case of arsenic poisoning. His scientific technique and testimony marks the beginning of modern forensic science. Today the field is divided into specialties such as biology (DNA analysis), chemistry, firearms and tool marks, questioned documents, toxicology, and pathology. This division is less than a half-century old. In Orfila's time the first to practice forensic science were doctors, chemists, lawyers, investigators, biologists, and microscopists with other skills and interests that happened to be of use to the legal system. Their testimony was and remains opinion testimony, something the legal system was slow to embrace. Early courts trusted swearing by oath—better still if oaths of others supported it. Eyewitnesses were also valued, even if their motives were less than honorable. Only in the last century has the scientific expert been integrated into the legal arena with a meaningful role. Essentials of Forensic Science is a distillation of the short history and current status of modern forensic science.

The set is divided into seven volumes:

☑ *Science versus Crime* by Max Houck, director of research — forensic science, West Virginia University; Fellow, American Academy of Forensic Sciences; formerly of the FBI (trace evidence analyst/anthropologist), working at the Pentagon and Waco. This book covers the important cases and procedures that govern scientific evidence, the roles of testimony and admissibility hearings, and how the law and scientific evidence intersect in a courtroom.

☑ *Blood, Bugs, and Plants* by Dr. R. E. Gaensslen, professor, forensic science; head of program and director of graduate studies; Distinguished Fellow, American Academy of Forensic

Sciences; former editor of the *Journal of Forensic Sciences.* This book delves into the many facets of forensic biology. Topics include a historical review of forensic serology (ABO blood groups), DNA typing, forensic entomology, forensic ecology, and forensic botany.

☑ *Drugs, Poisons, and Chemistry* by Dr. Suzanne Bell, Bennett Department of Chemistry, West Virginia University; Fellow of the American Board of Criminalistics; and Fellow of the American Academy of Forensics. This book covers topics in forensic chemistry, including an overview of drugs and poisons, both as physical evidence and obtained as substances in the human body. Also included is a history of poisoning and toxicology.

☑ *Trace Evidence* by Max Houck. This book examines the common types of microscopic techniques used in forensic science, including scanning electron microscopy and analysis of microscopic evidence, such as dust, building materials, and other types of trace evidence.

☑ *Firearms and Fingerprints* by Edward Hueske, University of North Texas; supervising criminalist, Department of Public Safety of Arizona, 1983–96 (retired); Fellow, American Academy of Forensic Sciences; emeritus member of American Society of Crime Laboratory Directors (ASCLD). This book focuses on how firearms work, how impressions are created on bullets and casings, microscopic examination and comparison, and gunshot residue. The examination of other impression evidence, such as tire and shoe prints and fingerprints, is also included.

☑ *Crashes and Collapses* by Dr. Tom Bohan, J. D.; Diplomate, International Institute of Forensic Engineering Sciences; Founders Award recipient of the Engineering Sciences Section, American Academy of Forensic Sciences. This book covers forensic engineering and the investigation of accidents such as building and bridge collapses; accident reconstruction, and transportation disasters.

☑ *Fakes and Forgeries* by Dr. Suzanne Bell. This book provides an overview of questioned documents, identification of handwriting, counterfeiting, famous forgeries of art, and historical hoaxes.

Each volume begins with an overview of the subject, followed by a discussion of the history of the field and mention of the pioneers. Since the early forensic scientists were often active in several areas, the same names will appear in more than one volume. A section on the scientific principles and tools summarizes how forensic scientists working in that field acquire and apply their knowledge. With that foundation in place the forensic application of those principles is described to include important cases and the projected future in that area.

Finally, it is important to note that the volumes and the set as a whole are not meant to serve as a comprehensive textbook on the subject. Rather, the set is meant as a "pocket reference" best used for obtaining an overview of a particular subject while providing a list of resources for those needing or wanting more. The content is directed toward nonscientists, students, and members of the public who have been caught up in the current popularity of forensic science and want to move past fiction into forensic reality.

# ACKNOWLEDGMENTS

I would like to extend my thanks to the RCBS Corporation for generously allowing the use of images of their firearms products and equipment.

I am particularly indebted to Chris Womack of the Department of Criminal Justice at the University of North Texas for her editorial assistance and diligent efforts in retyping the manuscript for this text.

My thanks as well to Frank Darmstadt, my editor, Dorothy Cummings, project editor, and the rest of the staff at Facts On File for their invaluable contributions to the completion and publication of this volume.

# INTRODUCTION

The goal of physical evidence preservation, collection, and examination is individualization, that is, to associate each piece of evidence with its responsible source. By so doing the forensic scientist may be able to answer the questions as to who, what, when, where, how, and why with regard to a crime.

Firearms and latent print evidence are in the uncommon category of physical evidence whose source can be individualized. Thus, a bullet or cartridge case can be identified as having been fired in a particular weapon to the exclusion of all similar weapons, and a fingerprint can be identified as having been left by a particular individual. Determining that a particular weapon was responsible for firing a fatal shot, though circumstantial, is often sufficient to convict someone, but actually putting that individual at the crime scene through fingerprints is the most powerful result. Of course, it is not always possible to find identifiable fingerprints at crime scenes or to find identifiable characteristics on bullets or cartridge cases.

Unfortunately misconceptions regarding the significance of not finding this evidence can lead to erroneous conclusions as to the events of a particular crime. Explanations typically abound as to why certain evidence is not present, and firearms and latent print evidence are no exception. The word to the wise is "absence of evidence is not evidence of absence."

It is widely accepted as unlikely, for example, that identifiable fingerprints will be found on firearms. Identifiable fingerprints will be found probably less than 10 percent of the time. When a suspect's fingerprints are not found on a murder weapon, however, defense attorneys often present this fact as an indication of their client's innocence.

Likewise, the forensic scientist must take care not to inflate the significance of the physical evidence that is present. For instance, investigation might turn up a partial fingerprint that cannot be positively identified as belonging to a particular individual. To describe such a print as "consistent with" having been made by a suspect without explaining the other possibilities (namely that numerous other persons could be responsible) would be misleading.

It is the responsibility of firearms and latent print examiners to properly represent their evidence within the limits of good science. The ability to do so is directly tied to their education, training, and experience. While ignorance may be blissful, it can have disastrous effects when people's lives hang in the balance of an examiner's written report and testimony.

Both firearms evidence examination and fingerprint comparison have had a long and interesting history. The role of fingerprints in human identification can actually be traced back several thousand years. The development of the science of fingerprint comparison, however, began in the early 19th century, as did the scientific examination of firearms.

*Firearms and Fingerprints* will trace these early beginnings and the icons that laid the groundwork for the current science. Attention will be given to the highly specialized education, training, and experience required to become a practitioner in the modern forensic laboratory. An examination of the capabilities and limitations of firearms and latent print evidence will provide insight into how these particular fields figure into the overall goal of crime scene reconstruction. Finally this book will look at future possibilities as these fields continue to evolve, as well as examine the legal challenges that have arisen recently as to the admissibility of both fingerprint and firearms identifications in court proceedings.

The author of this book has 33 years of combined experience as a forensic scientist, professor, and consultant. The case examples that are utilized in this volume are all cases in which the author has been personally involved. Thus, the reader will have the opportunity to learn about firearms and fingerprints from the perspective of someone who has and continues to be directly involved in these disciplines.

The author has also taught at both the middle and high school levels and is familiar with the learning needs of students at those levels. This experience is especially pertinent, given that this volume is directed to those students. The vast popularity of this subject matter at the university undergraduate and graduate levels has been addressed by numerous texts specifically designed for that level. Only a limited number of similar texts, however, are currently available to middle and high school students. This multivolume set seeks to help fill that gap and, thereby, better prepare students for advanced studies at the college and university level.

# Overview

This chapter introduces the reader to the wide variety of roles assumed by fingerprint and firearms examiners. These roles include crime laboratory duties, crime scene responsibilities, crime scene reconstruction, and providing court testimony. Developing the necessary qualifications that allow one to carry out these responsibilities will be presented. One of the goals of this chapter will be to give the reader an appreciation for the interrelationships of the various responsibilities and their overall dependency on having the proper combination of education and experience in order to be able to adequately carry them out.

## FIREARMS AND FINGERPRINTS IN THE CRIME LAB

The roles of firearms and fingerprint examiners in the crime laboratory are numerous and varied. Firearms examiners are frequently called upon to do many things that do not fall under the traditional heading of "firearms identification." Examples include serial number restoration with chemical etchants, gunshot residue analysis for barium nitrate, and shooting incident reconstruction. Similarly, fingerprint examiners must be proficient in specialized methods of photography, the application of chemical enhancers (such as luminol and leuco crystal violet), and the use of forensic light sources, as well as being proficient in fingerprint comparison.

The presence or absence of fingerprints on items of evidence submitted to the crime lab by scene investigators is a primary concern and thus constitutes a large part of the daily workload of the crime lab. This requires that fingerprint examiners examine most evidence first, before anyone else handles it. In some instances, such as when guns and ammunition are involved, both fingerprint examiners and firearms examiners examine the same evidence, but it is the fingerprint examiner who works with it first.

Contrary to portrayals in the movies and on television, fingerprints are not always easy to find on certain items of evidence. In the author's experience identifiable fingerprints are found on guns, knives, clubs, and the like in less than 10 percent of the cases. This is due to a number of factors including the surface characteristics of the weapon and the way in which the weapon was handled. On the other hand it is not uncommon to find some evidence of the handling of weapons in the form of partial fingerprint impressions, even though these partial impressions usually fall short of being identifiable to a specific individual.

Some types of evidence simply do not tend to retain any evidence of fingerprints, even when touched. Textured surfaces such as vehicle steering wheels, plastic milk jugs, and suitcase handles seldom show any sign of even having been touched. Other problems can include intense heat, humidity, and/or precipitation, which effectively destroy the fingerprints. Thus the probability of finding identifiable fingerprints on fired cartridge cases left at the crime scene, for example, is remote; the combination of the curved surfaces and the heat produced upon discharge tends to vaporize the fingerprints.

Fingerprints are of two basic types: visible and invisible. Visible fingerprints are termed *patent prints*. These fingerprints do not require any special enhancement, such as chemical treatment, in order to be seen. Plastic prints are a special type of visible fingerprints and consist of impressions found in paint, putty, and other pliable materials. Fingerprints that are not ordinarily visible are termed *latent fingerprints*.

Patent fingerprint *(Courtesy of the author)*

Latent fingerprints are only visible following the application of specialized lighting, powders, or chemicals. The photographs show an example of a patent print, a plastic print, and a latent print.

Fingerprint examiners typically begin their day in the crime lab by reviewing the new cases that have come in since their last shift. An evidence submission form accompanies all evidence that has been submitted to the crime lab. This form lists each item and specifies which items are to be examined for fingerprints.

In cases where a suspect has been developed, that suspect's fingerprints will also be submitted in the form of inked impressions on special white fingerprint cards. Using these, the examiner can make a direct comparison of any fingerprints found on the evidence with the suspect's prints on the fingerprint cards.

In the event that no suspect has been developed prior to submission of the evidence, any fingerprints found by the examiner will be placed into an automated fingerprint identification system (AFIS), and a computer search will be conducted. If the fingerprints are determined to be similar to any prints in the database, the examiner will then make a "manual" comparison; in other words, the examiner, not the computer,

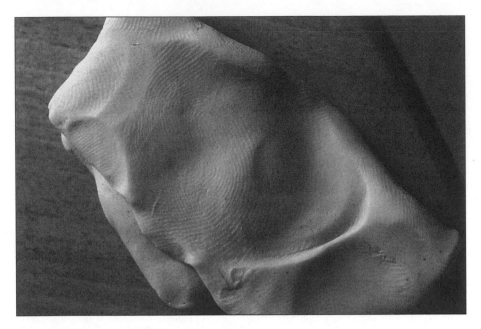

Plastic fingerprint *(Courtesy of the author)*

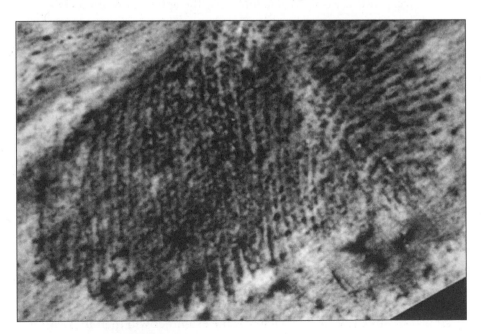

Latent fingerprint *(Courtesy of the author)*

visually compares each print identified by the computer against the suspect's known print to identify a match. If no identification can be made, the fingerprints go into an open case file in the database. They will remain there until either they are identified or the examiner removes them.

Fingerprint examiners use a wide variety of techniques, both physical and chemical, to develop and/or enhance fingerprints on a wide variety of surfaces. These will be discussed in chapter 3.

An additional crime lab role of fingerprint examiners is photographic documentation of the fingerprints that are located. Consequently the examiner must be well versed in the various aspects of photography. This particular duty is appropriate since the fingerprint examiner is really the only person who knows what areas of the prints are most important and hence must be visible in photographs that are made for documentation purposes.

Through the use of digital imaging, fingerprints found at crime scenes may be downloaded onto computer hard drives. By utilizing specialized software the examiner can then enhance the prints. Digital enhancement usually involves a combination of eliminating background

Latent fingerprint photography *(Courtesy of the author)*

interference, such as patterns or grains, and increasing contrast between the fingerprint and the substrate (the surface that the print is on). In this way faint prints that would be otherwise unidentifiable become clear enough to identify.

When the examiner is able to identify fingerprints as belonging to a particular individual, the next step is independent verification. This means that another examiner is called upon to review the prints (known and questioned) and either confirm or deny the original identification. The requirements for making fingerprint identifications will be discussed in a later section.

The purpose of verification is twofold. First, confirmation of all identifications is part of a crime lab's quality assurance program and serves to minimize the potential for false identifications. The second reason is that if the original examiner is unavailable when the case goes to court, the verifying examiner can step in as needed and testify as to the identification.

Fingerprint examiners are also sometimes required to work with partially decomposed bodies in an effort to identify the deceased. This task can require actually removing the skin from the cadaver's fingers and using various techniques to make the skin suitable for producing inked fingerprints, which in turn are used in the identification process. An admittedly gruesome aspect of this can include slipping the finger skin over the gloved fingers of the examiner in order to make an inked impression of each. Clearly this is not a job for the squeamish!

Fingerprint examiners are also on occasion called to court for the purpose of identifying individuals who are about to be sentenced. This is done to verify that the correct individual is being sentenced. The examiner will usually take inked impressions from the suspect during a court recess, compare them to known prints, and then take the witness stand to testify that the individual before the court is in fact the accused.

Large police agencies often have fingerprint technicians, in addition to fingerprint examiners. Fingerprint technicians assist fingerprint examiners by taking the inked fingerprint impressions from suspects in crimes, but fingerprint examiners may be responsible for taking the inked impressions of arrested persons themselves. To record these impressions the technician or examiner applies ink directly to the subject's hands, or

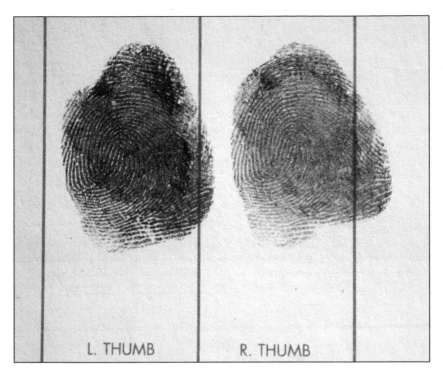

L. THUMB        R. THUMB

Portion of an inked fingerprint card *(Courtesy of the author)*

special inkless cards may be used. Individual fingers, as well as the palms and entire surface of the hands, are impressed onto the fingerprint cards, as shown in the photograph. These inked fingerprints are then entered into an AFIS database. This enables examiners to compare known fingerprints with latent fingerprints of unknown origin recovered at crime scenes. AFIS "hits" consist of lists of suspect prints exhibiting similarities to the prints entered into the database.

Firearms identification is similar to fingerprint examination only to the extent that both processes involve the comparison of known items with unknown items from the crime scene. Otherwise these are two entirely different fields of endeavor. For that reason two different individuals generally carry out firearms examinations and fingerprint examinations.

The term *firearms identification* is often used in conjunction with the term *tool mark identification*. In reality, much of firearms identification entails a specific area of tool mark identification. By definition a tool

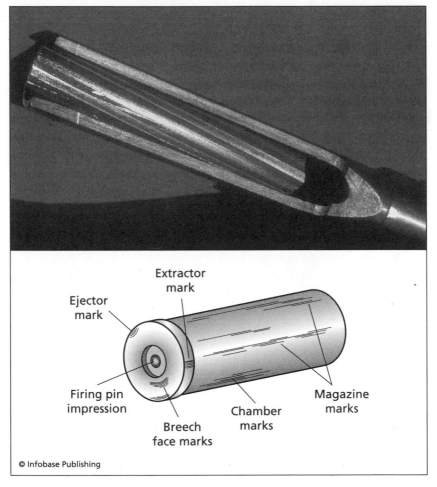

© Infobase Publishing

*Top:* Cutaway of a gun barrel *(Courtesy of the author)*
*Bottom:* Cartridge case markings

mark results from the contact of one surface with another, the harder of which is the "tool." Thus, in the case of a firearm and a bullet, the firearm (for instance the interior of the barrel) is the tool that produces tool marks on the surface of the bullet as it moves through the barrel upon discharge of the firearm. Likewise, the examination of firing pin impressions, magazine marks, extractor marks, ejector marks, breech face marks, and chamber marks on fired cartridge cases all constitute tool mark examinations.

Bullets and cartridge cases *(Courtesy of the author)*

The fact that firearms identification also involves examinations other than tool marks accounts for the distinction between the two areas. The analysis of gunpowder patterns on clothing, the determination of cartridge case ejection patterns, and the measurement of trigger pull or establishing bullet trajectory are examples. Likewise, weapons function testing, shot pellet pattern testing, and serial number restoration are additional non–tool mark comparison aspects of firearms identification.

Firearms identification is often referred to as "forensic ballistics" or just "ballistics." This is actually a misnomer, as ballistics is limited to the study of projectile behavior. Ballistics, in the true sense, includes three different aspects: interior ballistics (bullet behavior within the confines of the barrel), exterior ballistics (bullet behavior upon exiting the barrel), and terminal ballistics (bullet behavior upon impacting a target). Wound ballistics is a specialized area of terminal ballistics relating to the behavior of bullets striking human or animal targets.

Tool mark examination, on the other hand, is conducted to determine whether a tool mark was made by, or could have been made by, a particular tool. Tools commonly examined and compared with questioned (evidence) tool marks include hand tools—such as pliers, saws, screwdrivers, pry bars, hammers, and chisels—and power tools—such as drills, air chisels, chain saws, and reciprocating saws.

Thus, firearms and tool mark examinations have similarities and differences. If firearms and/or ammunition components are being examined, then the term *firearms examination* is most appropriate. Likewise, when marks produced by something other than a firearm are involved *tool mark examination* is appropriate. Since the majority of the work in a crime lab involves firearms and ammunition components, tool mark examinations might be considered a secondary discipline. At the New York City Police Department (NYPD) Crime Laboratory, for example, the firearms examiners do not presently carry out any tool mark examinations due to the heavy load of firearms-related work.

Firearms examiners are frequently asked to predict the type of firearm used to fire various ammunition components (such as bullets, cartridge cases, or shot cups) found at crime scenes. Having some idea of the firearm that was used in a crime allows investigators to know what type of weapon to be on the look out for. For example, being able to determine that the weapon used to fire a bullet found at the scene has polygonal rifling helps narrow the number of possible weapons.

In order to be able to test-fire weapons with missing parts, to identify certain weapons based on their special characteristics, and to make other comparisons, firearms examiners must have access to weapons collections. Finding a needed part for test-firing an antique rifle with a rolling block action or a shotgun barrel with a particular choke, for example, is easy when such a weapon is available in a reference collection. Ammunition reference collections must also be created and maintained to allow firearms examiners to be able to make various comparisons. Collections should include center fire and rim fire cartridges (primer located in the annular rim), as well as shot shells (including bird shot). Weapons and ammunition reference collections require regular inventory for security purposes. The larger a reference collection is, the greater the need for security. The Los Angeles County Sheriff's Department, for example, has more than 100,000 specimens in its firearms reference collection, making maintenance and inventory a formidable task.

The use of databases in firearms examinations also requires some tedious work in order to enter the necessary data. The markings left on fired bullets and cartridge cases found at crime scenes and recovered at autopsies must be entered into a national database called the National Integrated Bullet Identification Network (NIBIN) so as to allow examiners around the country to search the database to see if the same weapon that fired the bullets and/or cartridge cases they are examining was used in other crimes. Street gangs in particular are notorious for retaining weapons and using them in crime after crime. This information in the database allows firearms examiners to relate different crimes on the basis of the markings found on bullets and cartridge cases left at the crime scenes.

Firearms examiners are also called upon to attempt the restoration of obliterated serial numbers on firearms as well as other items ranging from automobile components and motorcycles to electronic equipment. This requires various specialized techniques that depend on the particular material the serial number is on and the degree to which obliteration has occurred.

## FIREARMS AND FINGERPRINTS AT THE CRIME SCENE

Due to the demands of the crime laboratory, not all examiners actually go to the crime scene to collect evidence and carry out testing in the field. Those laboratories where examiners do serve the dual role of laboratory analyst and scene investigator typically limit the on-scene aspect to major cases. Otherwise, there simply would be no way to get all the requested work done back at the lab.

Big city police departments, such as the NYPD and the Washington Metropolitan Police Department, have special crime scene investigation units whose sole responsibility is to go to the scene and collect the evidence for the laboratory examiners. When there are special needs at the crime scene, firearms and fingerprint examiners may be called in even though this may not be part of their normal routine.

With regard to fingerprints it is usually the responsibility of the persons assigned to the crime scene units to locate, develop, and lift latent prints at crime scenes. The actual comparison of crime scene prints with suspects' prints will usually be done in the crime lab by the fingerprint examiner.

Crime scene investigators are also trained to collect bullets, cartridge cases, and other ammunition components for examination by firearms examiners. Firearms examiners can be called in when special needs arise. For example, a sniper shooting involving a shot fired from a long distance that needs special bullet trajectory analysis may require a firearms examiner to come to the scene. This was the case in the investigation of the Beltway Sniper (see sidebar).

Crime laboratories in less populated jurisdictions can typically allow their examiners to devote time to crime scene investigations, in addition to their laboratory duties. These laboratories usually do not have the lab caseload demands that their big city counterparts have.

## The Beltway Sniper Case

In 2002 a sniper murdered a series of people who were refueling their vehicles at gas stations and convenience stores in the Washington, D.C., area, gripping area residents in fear for weeks. Members of the firearms identification unit of the Bureau of Alcohol, Tobacco and Firearms (ATF) came to the scenes of the various shootings in an effort to determine where the shots were fired from and to see if any other evidence could be found at the scenes.

The firearms analysts were able to conclude that a 223-caliber rifle was involved and that one weapon was responsible. They reached this conclusion by examining markings left on the bullets recovered from the victims. Once the weapon was recovered, it was positively identified using these same markings.

The "Beltway Sniper" was actually two men, John Muhammad and Lee Malvo, who fired a rifle from the trunk of their car. Malvo was implicated as a shooter through a fingerprint found on the weapon and a fingerprint found on a cartridge case near one of the scenes. Finding identifiable fingerprints on weapons and fired cartridge cases is pretty uncommon, making this a stroke of good luck for investigators. Muhammad and Malvo received the first of their convictions in 2004.

Small, local police agencies often call upon state and federal laboratories to send examiners to assist at crime scenes when the local agencies do not have their own examiners. Even larger agencies will call on Federal Bureau of Investigation (FBI) or Bureau of Alcohol, Tobacco, Firearms and Explosives (ATF) examiners to assist at crime scenes in high-profile cases. This is because the federal agencies sometimes have more resources and access to more specialized personnel and equipment than the state and local agencies do.

## THE RECONSTRUCTION OF CRIMES USING FIREARMS AND FINGERPRINT EVIDENCE

Shooting incidents can range from fairly simple events, such as when a single weapon is used to fire a single shot, to very complex situations involving multiple weapons used to fire multiple shots. A wide and varied array of mitigating circumstances may further add to the complexity of the incident. Regardless of the complexity, the same basic principles are utilized to reconstruct the events before, during, and after a shooting. A careful, logical approach can often take some of

Footwear impression *(Courtesy of the author)*

the "bite" out of what at first may appear to be a nearly overwhelming situation.

Shooting incident analysis and reconstruction are based on the application of a number of disciplines, some of which are firearms related and some of which are not. The firearms-related disciplines include external ballistics, firearms identification, and wound ballistics. Other disciplines, which are often utilized in shooting reconstructions, include bloodstain pattern interpretation, trace evidence, DNA, and footwear and tire tread examination as well as fingerprints. Shooting reconstruction also involves criminal investigation. Witness statements, business records, phone records, and other documentation are obtained through criminal investigation and help provide essential information for reconstructing the events of the crime.

It must be remembered that a shooting reconstruction is nothing more than a reasonable explanation, not a proposal of absolute fact. There is typically no way that the shooting reconstructionist will be able to state with complete certainty each and every detail associated with a shooting. There are simply too many variables involved. For example, the simple question as to how a shooter's feet or hands may have been positioned at some point during a shooting may certainly be approximated, but it is unlikely that their exact positions may be determined except in rare situations.

Reconstructions take into account all the available documentation (reports, affidavits, photos, videos, sketches, notes, and the like), the physical evidence, and witness accounts in order to develop a likely scenario that best fits all this information. It is critical that nothing be left without explanation in the proposed scenario if at all possible. Sometimes, of course, there are unexplainable things at scenes.

Reconstructions may be done at the scene or off-scene utilizing data collected by others. Obviously it is advantageous for the reconstructionist to have firsthand knowledge of the layout of the scene and the spatial arrangements of the various components, but this may not always be necessary or even possible. In the author's experience most shooting reconstructions have been done after the fact with no visit to the actual scene unless reconstruction was done well after the event in question. The success of this endeavor lies in the hands of the individuals who are gathering the information, documentation, and physical evidence at the scene and supplying it to the reconstructionist.

Reconstruction may incorporate reenactment. This reenactment may take on the form of live participants who are videotaped or photographed as they carry out a certain role, or computerized animations may be used. The obvious concern with any form of reenactment is that it pretty much fixes on a certain set of body positions and movements in order to provide the illustration being given. Sometimes it is a certain movement or body position that is the focus of a reconstruction. It is, in those instances, intended that no alternative positions be given equal consideration. This, however, is the exception rather than the rule.

Unlike some of their portrayals on television shows, actual firearms examiners and fingerprint examiners do not get involved in the interrogation and interviewing aspect of a case. Their role is strictly limited to working with the evidence. Firearms examiners might be called upon, for example, to determine the sequence of shots fired at the scene of a shooting. This could involve examining bullet holes in cars and looking at ricochet marks to determine the direction from which the shots were fired.

The presence or absence of fingerprints could play a key role in the reconstruction effort. For example, in the investigation of shooting deaths, the question of suicide versus homicide often comes up. If identifiable fingerprints actually happen to be present on a weapon and they do not belong to the victim, homicide might be indicated. On the other hand, if fingerprints are conspicuous by their absence, further investigation is warranted.

The reconstruction of a crime involves answering the following questions:

- Who?
- What?
- When?
- Where?
- How?

Reconstruction combines the results of the physical evidence examination and investigative efforts. A combination of crime scene observations and laboratory analyses are often necessary to solve the riddle. Firearms and fingerprint evidence, along with other types of physical evidence, play a key role in reconstructing the events associated with a crime.

## Conspicuous Absence

In a case the author investigated in the 1990s, the victim of a shotgun blast to the chest appeared to have shot himself. He was found on the floor of his residence with the shotgun lying nearby. A fired shot shell was found in the gun. A check of the gun failed to reveal any fingerprints. As previously explained, most of the time identifiable fingerprints will not be found on guns; however, in this case their absence was noteworthy.

The only way the victim could have shot himself was by grasping the end of the barrel of the gun with one hand and depressing the trigger with the other. The gun barrel was an ideal surface for leaving fingerprints: highly polished and covered in a light film of oil. It would have been impossible for the victim to grasp the barrel of the gun and not leave at least some evidence of fingerprints—partial prints, smudges, or smears. Investigators confirmed this by taking the gun and grasping the barrel in various ways and with varying degrees of force.

Further investigation revealed that the death was a homicide. Police later identified a suspect and obtained a search warrant for his residence. A search turned up items stolen from the victim's residence. The burglar apparently was surprised by the homeowner's early arrival from work, shot him with his own shotgun, then staged the murder to look like suicide. A hasty crime scene evaluation could have overlooked the critical missing fingerprint evidence to reach a conclusion of suicide.

## PUTTING IT ALL TOGETHER FOR THE JURY

The most difficult and by far the most important job for firearms and fingerprint examiners is the presentation of their findings in court. It is one thing to sit in the comfort of the crime lab and prepare a report—or even to be out at the crime scene carrying out tests and making determinations—but quite another to give testimony in court. Even the boldest, most self-assured individuals usually experience a world-class case of the butterflies when faced with the prospect of taking the witness stand.

The primary challenge is to present credible testimony in a clear, concise, and understandable manner. Another formidable challenge is to withstand cross-examination by the defense attorney. Defense attorneys seek to find weaknesses in the evidence being presented. Accordingly, the experts must not overstate their opinions or give testimony that is not based on good science.

At trial the expert first undergoes direct examination, in which the prosecutor takes the examiner step by step through the process he or she used to examine the forensic evidence related to the case. Meanwhile the defense attorney listens attentively, taking copious notes. The rules of discovery require the prosecution to reveal the general aspects of the expert's testimony well before the trial. Any unanticipated deviations or new revelations typically elicit objections from the defense attorney.

In cross-examination the defense attorney poses questions to the expert that will challenge the examiner's findings. This is when the firearms and fingerprint examiners really earn their money. The tactics used by defense attorneys vary with the personality of the individual, the case facts, and the perceived damage done by the expert's testimony during direct examination. While some attorneys will try to discredit the examiner's report by raising doubts about the expert's credentials, past testimony, and personnel records, attorneys with more skill and experience usually take other approaches. One is to try to establish rapport with the state's expert (the firearms or fingerprint examiner, in this case) and then use the state's expert to bring home certain points favorable to the defense. Another approach is to take each point made by the prosecution and offer alternative explanations. The expert is then confronted with the question of whether the alternative explanation is equally likely. This creates doubt and dilutes the effectiveness of the prosecution's presentation.

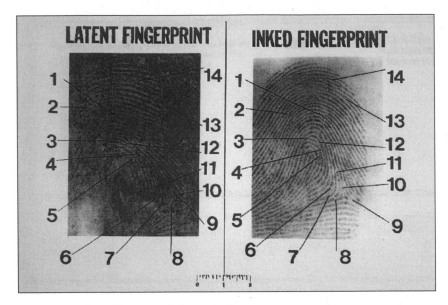

Fingerprint chart *(Courtesy of the author)*

The duty of the expert on the witness stand is to convince the members of the jury of his or her viewpoint. This can be a formidable task when the subject matter involves significant technical explanations and the jury is composed of individuals with little or no technical training. Experts must learn to present their findings in terms that can be understood by all. For example, in trying to explain why in the discharge of a firearm gunpowder particles travel further horizontally than soot particles, the firearms examiner can easily lose a jury by resorting to an explanation of mass, momentum, air friction, and the acceleration due to gravity. A better way of explaining the situation is to make an analogy with something most jurors are probably already familiar with. Thus, an explanation could be given that gunpowder and soot in horizontal flight could be likened to the coarse stream and fine mist settings of a garden hose. Most people are familiar with this example and understand that the coarse stream easily outdistances the fine mist.

How something is said can be as important as what is said. Testimony given in a tentative, weak voice suggests that the examiner is unsure of his or her findings. A strong, confident voice and eye contact with the members of the jury project a self-assured image that translates to believability. The expert must believe in the evidence results in order to be able to project this to the jury. This is analogous to one of the basic rules of commercial sales: You have to believe in your product, or no one will ever buy it.

Fingerprint examiners typically bring charts to court to help present their findings to the jury. These charts show the basis for their conclusion as to the fingerprint identification. The charts are poster size and are set up on an easel in front of the jury. The examiner refers to the charts as the explanation of the identification is given.

Firearms examiners use a variety of demonstrative exhibits, including photographs, diagrams, scale models, and computerized animation. These exhibits assist in both explaining the examinations conducted and presenting the theory of reconstruction of the shooting. Television and movies have caused jurors to come to expect a high-tech presentation and it is up to the expert to rise to the occasion. Given all the high-tech equipment and crime lab capabilities, this is not a real stretch to accomplish.

Firing pin impression *(Courtesy of the author)*

## HOW TO BECOME A FIREARMS OR FINGERPRINT EXAMINER

The basic educational requirements for firearms examiners and fingerprint examiners vary from agency to agency. College degrees, once the exception in these two fields, are rapidly becoming the norm. There are, however, still a few agencies that do not require a college degree for their firearms and fingerprint examiners.

Most agencies that require college degrees as a part of the minimum qualifications do not have specific degree requirements. Once again, however, there is a trend toward degrees in the sciences. The reason for this is twofold: Academic courses in the natural sciences are beneficial to firearms and fingerprint examiners both in the context of capably performing their duties and providing scientific testimony to the court.

Having a science degree also allows the firearms or fingerprint examiner to meet the same qualifications as other forensic scientists working in crime labs and, thus, qualify for the same salaries. Historically, firearms and fingerprint examiners have not enjoyed the same pay scales as other forensic scientists because they lacked science degrees.

Anyone setting out to become a firearms or fingerprint examiner would be best advised to obtain a degree in one of the natural sciences (biology, chemistry, or physics) or in forensic science. This both prepares the individual academically and maximizes the hiring opportunities when competing for a job with others who are less academically qualified.

Forensic science degrees are not typically designed specifically for firearms or fingerprint examination; they do provide, however, a broad education in all aspects of forensic science. An exception to this is a course of study in fingerprint comparison now offered by Marshall University in West Virginia. This is currently the only such program in the country.

Firearms examination continues to rely primarily on on-the-job training. Until 2002 firearms examination training was strictly done in house. Agencies hiring trainees for firearms examiner positions would assign the trainee to a senior examiner who would oversee the training according to a training program the agency had developed. Formal training programs used by police agencies were typically patterned after a recommended curriculum developed by the Association of Firearm and Tool Mark Examiners (AFTE). In 2002 the ATF opened the first firearms examination training academy in the nation. The academy is offered free of charge to police agencies throughout the country. Attendees must be sponsored by police agencies.

One of the problems with in-house training programs of any sort is the expenditure of personnel hours not related to casework for both the trainer and the trainee. To train an inexperienced individual to the level where he or she can take on casework responsibilities in firearms or fingerprints usually requires as much as two years. While the trainer is not entirely lost to duties other than training during this period, a significant amount of time is involved.

For this reason crime lab managers have been reluctant to hire trainees. Most job postings still seek experienced examiners. This has made entry into these fields difficult. With programs like the ones at Marshall University and the ATF academy, managers will doubtless become more open to hiring inexperienced trainees. This outcome will become even more likely as more of these programs come into being.

Another requirement for individuals in firearms and fingerprint examination work that is becoming increasingly more common is certification. As in other professions, certification is an effort to establish that an individual meets some minimum level of professional qualifications.

Certification in fingerprint examination has been in place for many years and is offered through the International Association for Identification (IAI). Would-be examiners must pass a written examination that focuses on actual comparison of questioned prints to known prints. Many agencies require their examiners to become certified by IAI as part of the conditions for employment. To date, no courts have required certification in order for a fingerprint examiner to be allowed to testify, but that could change.

Firearms certification, on the other hand, is a relatively new program that has been developed by AFTE. This is currently a strictly voluntary program, and no agencies or courts require it, although this also may change as the trend of requiring expert witnesses to have formal credentials continues to expand. Accreditation is a lab-wide program developed by the American Society of Crime Laboratory Directors (ASCLD) and administered through the Laboratory Accreditation

Board (ASCLD-LAB). This program accredits the entire laboratory operation (facility, procedures, and personnel). The argument for AFTE certification and IAI certification, as opposed to ASCLD-LAB accreditation, is that if an examiner leaves the accredited lab to go to work at an unaccredited lab, the accreditation does not follow him or her, while certification does.

So, why all the fuss about accreditation and certification? It comes down to increasing scrutiny by courts on the credentials of individuals passing themselves off as "experts." These accreditation and certification programs have been borne out of the need to demonstrate scientific competency to the court.

As of 2002 more than half of the 350 crime labs in the country were accredited by ASCLD-LAB. While a majority of the fingerprint examiners throughout the country were then certified by IAI, only a small percentage of the firearm examiners had sought and obtained AFTE certification. Several states, including Texas and New York, have passed laws that require crime laboratories that analyze physical evidence and present their findings in court to be accredited. This trend will no doubt continue to spread.

Accreditation and certification programs are not a one-time event. Re-accreditation must take place every five years, and maintaining certification requires ongoing training. The quality assurance programs of most laboratories also require trainees to pass competency tests before they perform independent casework and require all examiners to pass ongoing proficiency testing as the years go by.

In summary anyone considering a career in fingerprints or firearms should first acquire a degree in some general area of science or in forensic science. Once they are hired by a law enforcement agency, beginning examiners should plan on an extended period of training that may or may not include mandatory certification. They should also expect to be required to pass annual proficiency tests and undergo peer review of both their casework and their court testimony.

## CONCLUSION

This chapter has offered the reader a glimpse into the wide-ranging roles of firearms and fingerprint examiners. Examiners in both disciplines must have sound academic backgrounds in the natural sciences and significant experience in order to perform at the highest level. The ability to carry out laboratory analyses and conduct field examinations forms the basis for being able to reconstruct events associated with crimes under investigation. The culmination of these efforts is the ability to articulate their meaning to a jury in a clear and understandable manner.

# 2

# A Brief History of Firearms and Fingerprints and the Scientists Involved

This chapter will provide the reader with a brief overview of the histories of firearms and fingerprints with a mention of some of the individuals who have played key roles in their respective development. The evolution of firearms has taken place over more than 200 years. It has been directly tied to the Industrial Revolution and the ongoing advances in manufacturing techniques, metallurgy, and pyrotechnics (for example, gunpowder).

Fingerprint technology has also evolved in the 100 years since its acceptance as a valid means of personal identification. The reader will be introduced to some of the more notable individuals who have helped shape modern methods of fingerprint analysis, as well as to some of the more significant technological advances.

## FIREARMS AND THE EVIDENCE THEY PROVIDE

A firearm is a weapon that is capable of firing a projectile and using an explosive charge as a propellant. The broadest category of firearms includes two types: handguns and long guns. Handguns are designed to

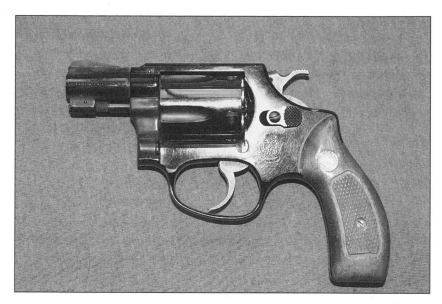

Revolver *(Courtesy of the author)*

Semiautomatic pistol *(Courtesy of the author)*

be fired while held in the hand, and long guns are designed to be fired from the shoulder.

Handguns include revolvers and pistols, examples of which appear in the accompanying photographs. Pistols are either semiautomatic (auto-loading) or fully automatic (machine pistol). The difference is that a semiautomatic pistol requires that the trigger be pulled for each shot, while a fully automatic continues to fire until all its ammunition is expended once the trigger is pulled and held. Pistols use magazines, sometimes erroneously referred to as "clips," to feed cartridges into their actions. Revolvers rely upon a rotating cylinder to hold cartridges and place them into a firing position. Revolvers are classed as either single action or double action. Single action means that the hammer must be manually cocked in order to fire the weapon. Double action means the hammer is cocked and the cylinder simultaneously rotated as the trigger is pulled.

Pistol actions function by stripping a cartridge from the magazine, seating it in the chamber, firing the cartridge, extracting the fired cartridge case, and ejecting it from the weapon. Each of these events potentially leaves identifiable tool marks on the cartridge case.

Long guns include rifles, shotguns, machine guns, and submachine guns. Rifles and shotguns can have a variety of actions including bolt action, lever action, and semiautomatic. Submachine guns and machine

Rifle *(Courtesy of the author)*

Shotgun *(Courtesy of the author)*

guns are capable of fully automatic fire. The difference between machine guns and submachine guns is that machine guns fire rifle cartridges and submachine guns fire pistol cartridges. Examples of a typical rifle and shotgun are shown in the photographs.

Handguns and long guns, with the exception of most shotguns, have spiral grooves cut or formed into the interior surface of the barrel. These grooves, called rifling, are designed to impart a spin to the bullet as it moves down the barrel upon discharge of the weapon. This spin stabilizes the bullet in flight to improve accuracy and increase the effective range. The areas between the barrel grooves are known as "lands." There are an equal number of lands and grooves in a gun barrel and typically ranges from two to 16. The grooves in the interior of a gun barrel are best described as in the shape of a helix (see the illustration on page 8). Various methods are used to create the rifling. Traditional methods involve cutting using hooks, carbide buttons, or broaches, while more recent methods rely on hammer forging or electrochemical etching.

The direction of twist of the lands and grooves may be either clockwise (to the right) or counterclockwise (to the left). The number and widths of lands and grooves, the direction of twist, and the degree of twist are among the class characteristics of a given make and model of weapon.

Degree of twist is the rate at which the rifling creates bullet spin per unit length. Common rates of twist for small arms would be 1:12 or 1:14 in regards to the number of bullet revolutions per inch of barrel length; in other words, one turn in 12 inches (30.5 cm) versus one turn in 14 inches (35.6 cm) (even though the barrel may not actually be that long).

The diameter of the barrel from land to land is the caliber of a weapon, another class characteristic. People sometimes confuse caliber with cartridge designation. For example, 9 mm Luger, 38 special, and 357 Magnum are designations for specific cartridge configurations. The

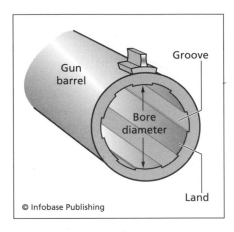

© Infobase Publishing

Caliber (bore diameter)

calibers of the weapons that fire these cartridges are all essentially the same, however. Caliber determination is illustrated in the diagram.

Shotguns, on the other hand, are usually smooth bore (without lands and grooves). Since shotguns usually fire small spherical pellets, they do not need the spin stabilization provided by rifling. Shotguns may also be used to fire "slugs" (single, large projectiles), in which case spin stabilization is desirable. This may be accomplished by having spiral grooves cast into the body of the slug itself. There are also shotguns with true rifling in the barrels.

Rather than by caliber most shotgun barrels are distinguished according to "gauge." Commonly encountered gauges include 12, 16, 20, and 28. The gauge designation is a holdover from old English terminology. Gauge represents the number of lead shot of a particular diameter to the pound. Thus, a 12-gauge shotgun barrel has a diameter such that 12 lead shot of that same diameter would weigh one pound. Since a 16-gauge shotgun represents a barrel diameter equivalent to 16 shot to the pound, a 12-gauge shotgun has a greater diameter than a 16-gauge, which is greater than 20, and so on. The exception is 410 shotguns, which are actually designated as to caliber (0.410 inch [1.05 cm] diameter) rather than gauge.

## FIREARMS EXAMINATION EMERGES AS A DISCIPLINE

The emergence of firearms as a discipline can probably be credited to Henry Goddard during the mid-19th century in England. Goddard was credited with recognizing the potential of firearms-related evidence to help place an individual at the scene of a shooting. This section will review some of Goddard's accomplishments in that realm.

## The Contributions of Henry Goddard in London

One of the early pioneers in the field of criminal investigation, Henry Fielding (1707–54), is credited with developing the Bow Street Runners in England, forerunners of modern detectives. Fielding is also well known as a novelist and playwright. One of the last of the Bow Street Runners, Henry Goddard (1800–83), is recognized as one of the first individuals to recognize the potential of firearms evidence as an aid in identifying the criminals involved.

In 1835 Goddard successfully identified a murderer by using a bullet recovered from the body of the victim at autopsy. In those days bullets were produced by melting lead and pouring it into two-piece molds. Most individuals used their own lead and bullet molds to produce bullets for their guns.

## Food for Thought: Individualization

In 1835 the level of investigative sophistication was often relatively primitive, as one might expect. But one still wonders how Goddard failed to recognize, through basic reasoning, that a very large question remained as to the validity of his process of "individualization." Noticing a defect in the bullet that probably resulted from manufacture, Goddard concluded that the suspect's bullet mold was the only mold that could have been used. Can you foresee the potential problem with Goddard's conclusion? If you are asking yourself about other similar molds, you are on the right track.

Of course, Goddard got a confession from the suspect, but what if he had not? Furthermore, people sometimes confess to crimes they did not commit. What if the suspect, despite his confession, was not the murderer? A firearms examiner of today would certainly investigate how the molds were produced and find out whether other molds bearing similar defects could reasonably be expected to exist.

Goddard examined the bullet recovered from the victim and noticed that there was a defect in the surface of the bullet that appeared to be the result of manufacture and not from the gun barrel or the impact of the bullet with the victim. Since it was anticipated that the shooter would have made his own bullet, Goddard predicted that a bullet mold might provide the necessary evidence as to who was responsible.

When a suspect was finally identified, Goddard went to his residence and quickly located a bullet mold with a corresponding defect. By casting several bullets using the seized mold and comparing them with the bullet from the victim, Goddard was able to show that that particular mold had made the fatal bullet. Ultimately, when confronted with the evidence, the suspect confessed to the murder.

## EARLY FIREARMS EXAMINATIONS IN THE UNITED STATES

During the U.S. Civil War firearms examination was used in several notable cases. One such case was the shooting of Confederate general Thomas "Stonewall" Jackson. In 1863 General Jackson was shot by what was believed to be one of his own men during the Battle of Chancellorsville. The bullet struck the general in his right arm necessitating its amputation. Pneumonia set in and ultimately caused the general's death.

Following the amputation surgeons recovered the bullet. The bullet was examined by Confederate officers, who determined its caliber and design, both of which were consistent with Confederate weapons and inconsistent with Union weapons. Thus, it was confirmed that the general had, in fact, been the victim of "friendly fire."

The following year, 1864, Union general John Sedgwick was shot dead by a Confederate sniper from an estimated distance of 800 yards. The fatal bullet was removed from Sedgwick's body and examined. Based upon its hexagonal shape and caliber, it was determined to be consistent with English Whitworth rifles imported and used by the Confederacy.

These developments alerted both the legal and the scientific communities to the potential evidentiary value of firearms evidence. While these initial efforts were limited to the recognition and comparison of class characteristics (characteristics common to two or more similar items), they form the basis for the initial examinations still used by modern examiners. The next section relates to the comparison of another type of class characteristics: general rifling marks.

## PROFESSOR ALEXANDRE LACASSAGNE: A PIONEER IN BLOODSTAIN ANALYSIS

Alexandre Lacassagne (1844–1921) was a professor at the University of Lyons, France. He was the first scientist to study bullet markings and their relationship to specific weapons. In 1889 in France, Professor Lacassagne removed a bullet from a corpse. He noted that the rifling impressions on the bullet were from a weapon with seven lands and seven grooves. A number of possible suspects were rounded up and their weapons turned over to Professor Lacassagne for examination. Ultimately, the professor determined that only one of the submitted weapons had seven lands and seven grooves. On that basis the gun's owner was convicted of murder.

This finding was significant in that it was the first time that rifling marks on fired bullets had been used to exclude certain weapons. Thus, the foundation for modern firearms identification, as applied to projectiles, had been laid.

Are there any potential flaws in the basis on which the gun's owner was convicted? As noted in the discussion on firearm types, the number of lands and grooves in a gun barrel does vary; however, two other questions should have been considered in Lacassagne's examination: How many other guns with seven lands and seven grooves exist, and how many could have been used to fire the fatal shot? Another concern would be the fact that the direction of twist of the rifling could either be to the left or the right. Thus, if numbers of lands and grooves alone were considered, a serious error could have been involved in the conviction.

In 1898 in Berlin, chemist Paul Jeserich was provided with a bullet from a murder victim along with the suspect's revolver. He was asked to see if he could determine whether the revolver was used to fire the fatal bullet. Jeserich unknowingly stood at the brink of historical prominence as he proceeded to test-fire the revolver, prepare photomicrographs of the surfaces of both test and evidence bullets, and compare the microscopic markings on the bullet surfaces to each other.

As fate would have it, Jeserich did no follow-up work and made no further effort to develop his methodology. Thus, his place in firearms identification history is analogous to a modern-day musician who goes no further than getting one song on the record charts and subsequently becomes known as a "one hit wonder." Nonetheless, Jeserich brought firearms identification closer to its modern-day counterpart by recognizing the importance of individual characteristics (accidental, random characteristics) as the appropriate means for establishing identification of bullets to specific firearms.

## THE BROWNSVILLE RIOT AND CARTRIDGE CASE COMPARISONS

In 1907 several U.S. Army infantry soldiers allegedly fired 150–200 shots from their army-issue rifles at various targets within the town of Brownsville, Texas. This was all supposed to have taken place within an approximately 10-minute period during the night. The facts were and continue to be very much in question. It was never confirmed that any of the accused soldiers actually fired a shot.

What was significant about the incident is that it marked the first shooting episode in the United States in which an effort was undertaken to examine fired cartridge cases and to attempt to match them to a specific rifle. This task fell to the Frankfort Arsenal in Kentucky. A total of 39 fired cartridge cases, some fired bullets, and numerous rifles were shipped to the arsenal for examination and comparison.

The arsenal staff devised a method of comparing markings on the fired cartridge cases to test-fired cartridge cases from the rifles. Ultimately, four of the rifles were determined to have been used to fire the cartridge cases. No conclusions were reached regarding the fired bullets, but the government published a report entitled "Study of the Fired Bullets and Shells in Brownsville, Texas, Riot." This extensive report marks a milestone in the forensic examination of firearms and ammunition components as the first recorded instance of cartridge case examination and comparison.

## PROFESSOR VICTOR BALTHAZARD AND BULLET COMPARISON IN FRANCE

The various other aspects of firearms identification were not really recognized for their potential value in solving crimes until the early 20th century. In 1913 Victor Balthazard, a professor at the Sorbonne, in Paris, published what was clearly a monumental paper on firearms identification ("Identification des Projectiles de Revolver en Plomb Nu" in Volume 148 of *Comptes Rendus de l'Académie des Sciences*). In this article Balthazard discussed bullet comparison and also made reference to the fact that marks left on cartridge cases by firing pins, breech faces, ejectors, extractors, chambers, and magazines were all of potential value in identifying the responsible firearm.

Balthazard devised a method of photographing the lands and grooves of the bullets and enlarging the photographs so that the microscopic markings left by the gun barrel could be compared. Balthazard's paper remained virtually unnoticed due to the world's focus on the approach of World War I.

## CALVIN GODDARD AND THE BEGINNINGS OF MODERN FIREARMS EXAMINATION IN THE UNITED STATES

Once people began to realize the significance of Balthazard's paper, the field of firearms identification began to emerge. Probably the most significant individual to put his shoulder to the task was Calvin Goddard, an American physician. Goddard is considered responsible for perfecting the comparison microscope, a mainstay in the comparison of firearms ammunition components.

Goddard worked with a team of other American scientists in developing the science of firearms identification: Phillip Gravelle, Charles Waite, and John Fisher. Following Waite's death in 1926, Goddard became the leader of the group and is recognized as the Father of Firearms Identification. Waite made a very significant contribution himself, however. He visited various firearms manufacturers to get exemplar weapons and to catalog data associated with the various weapons. Ultimately, he put together the first firearms reference collection of significance in this country.

A firearms reference collection is an essential part of the resources needed in firearms examinations. Such a collection allows the examiner to replace missing parts from evidence firearms so that test-firing may be accomplished. It also permits the examiner to verify when modifications have been made to evidence firearms.

## FINGERPRINTS: WHAT THEY ARE
## AND HOW THEY ARE PRODUCED

A fingerprint can be defined as a replica of the friction ridges of the skin cast on a surface. Despite the name *fingerprints,* these friction ridges are also produced by the palms, the toes, and the soles of the feet. While there are a few exceptions among those who are physically impaired, everyone has the friction ridges that produce fingerprints. Friction ridge patterns are affected by genetics, but even twins with identical genes have different fingerprints. Since a print of one finger has never been known to duplicate the print of another finger, even in the case of identical twins, it is possible to identify an individual with just one impression. Despite factors such as the environment and aging, one's friction ridges do not change, thus making fingerprints a permanent record of an individual throughout life.

To understand the concepts of what kind of prints exist, it is necessary to be able to recognize what a print is composed of. An invisible print, or latent print, is created when the friction ridges deposit materials on a surface that are generally invisible to the naked eye. A print is mostly made up of sweat. The primary component of sweat is water. Therefore, if a fingerprint were left alone, it would eventually dry.

There are also solid components of a fingerprint, including organic compounds like amino acids, glucose, proteins, and fatty acids as well as inorganic components like potassium, sodium, ammonia, and chloride salts. The basic premise of fingerprinting is to make a chemical react with a property in the fingerprint to make it visible. "Developing" a fingerprint is the process of making it visible.

An inked print refers to a print that is taken from a person and recorded directly onto a fingerprint card, as previously described. The correct procedure for obtaining an inked fingerprint is simple. Ink is placed on the area to be printed—the finger, for example—which is then rolled onto a card. The most common fingerprint card allows rolled prints to be taken from all 10 fingers. Using this method, prints can also be obtained from a palm or foot. The fingerprint cards are then filed away, usually by the agency that obtained the print, for comparison purposes when a print for evidence turns up. The person taking an inked print must be careful not to use too much ink and not to press too hard on the print card. Doing either will cause the print to smudge, making it useless. "Inkless" systems, which utilize ink that easily wipes off, eliminate these concerns altogether. Chemically treated paper systems use no ink whatsoever. Livescan systems use biometric hardware to create direct digital images from the suspect's finger surfaces.

Although new technology is making inked prints, of any type, a thing of the past, there is still some use for them. Agencies that do not have access to fingerprint databases may rely solely on fingerprint cards for comparison purposes. Smaller agencies that do not have the funds to run computer databases will continue to rely on manual methods for fingerprint comparison.

Evidence often involves latent prints. There are three broad categories of latent prints: plastic, or impression, prints; contaminated, or visible, prints; and latent, or invisible, prints. The term *latent prints* can refer to all three of these categories, as a whole, or specifically to invisible prints. As shown in chapter 1, plastic, or impression, prints are created when a finger touches pliable material, such as a newly painted surface, a layer of dust, putty, or adhesive tape. Contaminated, or visible, prints occur after a finger, contaminated with foreign matter, like blood, touches a clean surface, as shown in the photograph. Lastly, latent, or invisible, prints refer to the prints that are left as a result of the small amounts of perspiration and oil that are found on friction ridges.

Not all latent prints are able to be developed. The quality of latent prints relies on numerous conditions. The first condition to be considered is the surface that the print is deposited on. Plastic prints will last for years if undisturbed. Invisible prints on smooth surfaces, like glass or porcelain, can be developed after a similar period of time. Prints left on porous material like paper, however, are more variable in how long they can survive. It is possible that prints left on documents will fade or deteriorate. This can happen if they are subject to high humidity or become wet. Otherwise, invisible prints left on paper are fairly stable and can be developed years after they were left.

The second condition affecting the quality of latent prints is the nature of the material contaminating the fingerprint. Visible prints

Bloody print *(Courtesy of the author)*

left by powder, dust, or soot are easily destroyed, whereas prints left in blood, ink, or oil will last longer periods of time under favorable conditions.

The third condition to consider is the person leaving the fingerprint. One must consider any physical or occupational defects of the subject leaving the print. For example, the fingerprints of an individual who has worked with their hands, like a bricklayer, may have very unusual qualities. Their fingerprints are not destroyed, but typically they do contain several points that can be used as identification factors, such as calluses.

A fourth condition to consider is how the object bearing the prints was handled. If a suspect picks up a glass and the glass slips, it is possible that the print will be a bit off. This is because the distance between friction ridges is very small, and the ridge detail was lost.

The final condition is with regard to latent print quality, especially when dealing with contaminated or visible prints, is the amount of material contaminating the fingerprint. The friction ridges that make up fingerprints are basically a series of ridges and valleys. If too much of a contaminant—blood, for example—lies on the friction ridges, it will fill these valleys, resulting in a smudged print. These prints are of little or no value as fingerprint evidence.

At times it may seem very difficult to find a fingerprint; however, they are of such value that the investigating officer should take the time to recover any prints left behind. The officer should search all areas surrounding the crime scene thoroughly and initially collect as many prints as possible. It may be of assistance to shine a flashlight at an oblique angle to the surface being examined.

The fact that a glove may have been worn should not be of concern, as it is very possible that the glove itself may leave a print that is unique to it. Additionally, it may be possible to develop a fingerprint left on the inside of a glove recovered at a crime scene, as was the case in a 1996 burglary of an office building in Los Angeles, where the clumsy burglar left his rubber gloves. In this case the observant police officer noticed a pair of rubber gloves left inside the office building. The officer stored them as evidence in the hope that they might reveal the perpetrator. Using a chemical method, the investigator was able to develop a print detailed enough to obtain a conviction.

An officer investigating a crime scene should also pay close attention to areas that are commonly touched. If the crime occurred in a vehicle, the investigator should look on areas like the back of the rearview mirror, on buttons, the trunk lid, and steering wheel. If the crime scene is in a residence, less obvious places such as the undersides of toilet seats, handles of dresser drawers, and the backs of movable cabinets should not be ignored. It may help to have someone familiar with the area, like the resident, walk through so they can determine if anything is out of place.

Lastly, if there is any doubt, the investigator should always err on the side of caution and lift the print, because the fingerprints can always be ruled out as the victim's. Once destroyed, however, the evidence will be impossible to recover. After the fingerprints are collected as evidence, the investigator will need to compare them to other prints, possibly inked prints, to determine if they are a match.

To make a fingerprint match, a fingerprint examiner uses a combination of ridge characteristics, or "points," collectively known as "minutiae." The characteristics are ridge endings, bifurcations, lakes or deltas, independent ridges, dots or islands, spurs, and crossovers. A bifurcation is when a single ridge splits into two ridges. Ridge endings occur at the point at which a ridge ends. Delta regions are roughly oval-shaped areas where ridges flowing in different directions meet. Dots resemble pinpoints, and islands, which are slightly larger than dots, are isolated ridges. Dots and islands are local ridge characteristics that occur at either a ridge bifurcation or a ridge ending. Spurs resemble their namesake, the spurs worn by horse riders. Crossovers are ridges that cross other ridges.

## RIDGE CHARACTERISTICS

An examiner must be able not only to recognize what type of print a particular sample is or what category it fits into but also to identify, or match, at least 12 points. Fingerprint matching techniques can be placed into two categories: minutiae based and correlation based. Minutiae-based techniques first find minutiae points and then map their relative placement on the finger. However, there are some difficulties when using this approach. It is difficult to extract the minutiae points accurately when the fingerprint is of low quality. Also this method does not take into account the pattern of ridges and furrows.

The correlation-based method is able to overcome some of the difficulties of the minutiae-based approach; however, it has its own shortcomings. Correlation-based techniques require the precise location of a registration point and are affected by image translation and rotation (that is, the moving of one print relative to the one being compared).

Another problem that examiners must overcome is print size. Because there is no standard requirement of print size for positive identification, the print need only be large enough to contain the necessary points of individuality. Therefore, if the examiner can determine the "necessary" number of points, the print will suffice.

The fundamental benefits of fingerprint identification are permanence and individuality. It is these two characteristics that make the science of fingerprinting appropriate for individual identification and, thus, an excellent source of evidence for law enforcement.

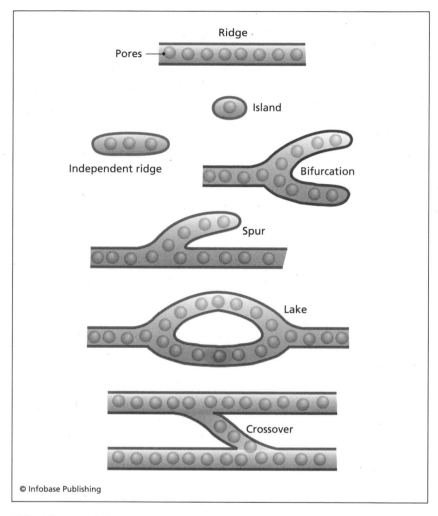

Ridge characteristics

When developed and processed correctly, fingerprints have obtained convictions on numerous cases. In the roughly 100 years that fingerprints have been used for identification purposes, no one has managed to falsify the claim of uniqueness by showing that fingers of two persons had identical fingerprints. Furthermore, other than growth and scarring, no one has shown that the distinctive characteristics of one person's fingerprints changed over time. This is why fingerprint examination, or dactylography, is such a reliable science.

## JOHANNES PURKINJE AND THE FIRST ATTEMPT AT FINGERPRINT CLASSIFICATION

Fingerprinting owes its prominence to certain icons whose research and discipline greatly advanced the field. These researchers took great time to study, take personal notes, and ultimately invent this new field but were never rewarded by seeing their work benefit anyone. Each one nonetheless contributed to advance the field.

Johannes Evangelista Purkinje, also known as, Jan or John Purkinje, is one of these scientists who advanced the field of fingerprinting. He was born in 1787 in what was Czechoslovakia. Although Purkinje's background was in physiology, he contributed to the field of criminology.

Purkinje was a professor at the University of Breslau in Germany from 1823 to 1850. While there he was a pioneer in establishing laboratory training in many German universities. In 1823 Purkinje named nine standard types of fingerprint patterns and outlined a broad method of classification. As Purkinje put it, "After innumerable observations, I have found nine important varieties of patterns of rugae and sulci, though the lines of demarcation between the types are often obscure." *Rugae* refer to ridges and *sulci* to furrows (the area between the ridges). He delineated the following patterns: transverse curve, central longitudinal stria, oblique stripe, oblique loop, almond whorl, spiral whorl, ellipse, circle, and double whorl. Although his system of classification is not used today, Purkinje was the first to recognize these patterns and classify them into a system.

## HENRY FAULDS AND WILLIAM HERSCHEL AND THE "WHO WAS FIRST?" CONTROVERSY

As is frequently the case in the history of scientific developments, there were several individuals working independently of one another who played somewhat equal roles as early proponents of fingerprint technology. These situations result in some degree of controversy as to who should receive the credit. The pioneering work of Henry Faulds and William Herschel in fingerprint technology serves as an example of the controversy that often arises as to "who was first."

Henry Faulds is another scientist who publicly declared his beliefs about the possibilities of using fingerprints. Faulds was born in Scotland on June 1, 1843, and grew up in a small town called Beith. Although he had humble beginnings, he would rise above them to be one of the first pioneers in fingerprinting.

Faulds studied mathematics and logic at Glasgow University. Four years later he decided to pursue medicine at Anderson College. Faulds was a doctor, and his passion was working as a medical missionary. He started missionary work in India but after a disagreement with the superintendent resigned one year later. In 1874 Faulds moved to Tokyo, Japan. He initially worked as a medical missionary but by 1875 was able to establish Tsukiji Hospital. While there Faulds introduced methods to combat typhoid and lectured on surgical complications. He became fluent in Japanese and taught at the local university. He was also responsible for founding the Tokyo Institute for the Blind that exists to this day. Faulds developed a system of raised script to allow blind people to read. This script was a forerunner of the modern-day Braille system.

While in Japan Faulds discovered fingerprints on ancient pottery. The fingerprints, left by their makers, fascinated him, and Faulds began extensive research. His research included many experiments to reveal the permanent uniqueness of fingerprints. In one experiment Faulds even attempted to remove his own fingerprints with emery paper and chemicals but discovered that they just grew back in the same pattern.

Faulds conducted a study on "skin furrows" and predicted its forensic application. He even forecast that fingerprints would one day be transmitted by phototelegraphy, which could be the precursor to the modern-day AFIS system. A related pair of incidents prompted Faulds to help develop fingerprint identification for criminals. A thief climbed a wall near his house and left sooty fingerprints on its whitewashed surface. When the police arrested a suspect, Faulds asked them if he could take fingerprints from their prisoner. He found that the fingerprints he took from the suspect did not match those on the wall and advised the police that they had detained the wrong man. Another suspect was taken into custody. This time the suspect's prints matched, and he confessed to the crime. This was the first recorded occasion when both innocence and guilt were proven by the use of fingerprints. This incident is what gave Faulds the confidence and perseverance to continue with his beliefs and studies.

In October 1880 Faulds became the first person to publicly suggest fingerprints as a method of identification when he published an article in *Nature* magazine. In that paper he made two important observations: "(1) When bloody finger-marks or impressions on clay, glass etc., exist, they may lead to the scientific identification of criminals, and (2) A common slate or smooth board of any kind, or a sheet of tin, spread over very thinly and evenly with printer's ink, is all that is required [to take fingerprints]." This was the first recorded suggestion that fingerprints could be used to locate criminals, and how it might be done.

Faulds not only recognized the importance of fingerprints as a means of identification, but he devised a method of classification as well. Additionally, through his experiments Faulds was the first to discover that fingerprints do not change throughout one's life. He forwarded an explanation of his classification system and a sample of the forms he had designed for recording inked impressions to Sir Charles Darwin. Darwin, in advanced age and ill health, informed Faulds that he could be of no assistance to him but promised to pass the materials on to his cousin, Francis Galton. In 1886 Faulds returned to England due to his wife's illness. While in England Faulds hoped to convince Scotland Yard that his system was superior to any previously used. Scotland Yard declined his offer but later regretted the decision. In fact, it was not until 1901 that the British began using fingerprints to identify potential criminals.

In the meantime the discovery of the use of fingerprints for criminal identifications was often credited to others, such as William Herschel, William Henry, and Galton. Faulds died in 1930, receiving no recognition for his contribution to the field of dactylography. In fact, it took well over 50 years for many to see that Faulds was an influential person in the field of dactylography.

Around the same time that Faulds was making his discoveries, William Herschel was also trying to break into the field of fingerprinting. Herschel was born in 1833 and began studying fingerprints in 1858. In the 1850s Herschel was the British chief administration officer in the Hooghly District in Bengal, India. Herschel is credited with being the first European to recognize the value of fingerprints for identification purposes. In July 1858 Herschel had a local businessman, Rajyadhar Konai, impress his handprint on the back of a contract. Herschel stated that he did this to "frighten him out of all thought of repudiating his signature." The businessman was impressed with Herschel's business skills, and Herschel was fond of his new discovery, so Herschel decided to require palm prints with all contracts. Herschel's use of fingerprints was not used to prove or disprove identity but rather to prevent locals from trying to break contracts. Herschel began collecting, as keepsakes, the fingerprints from these contracts and also of his friends and relatives. He took note of how each impression was unique to the individual and observed that the patterns did not change over time.

Herschel came to realize that fingerprints could be used to prove or disprove someone's identity. His fingerprinting ideas were not implemented until 1877–78, however, when he was finally able to administer their official use under his own authority. During that period Herschel had government pensioners in his region "sign" for their monthly payments with fingerprints. At the registry of deeds, landowners impressed fingerprints to authenticate their transactions. At the courthouse convicts were forced to fingerprint their jail warrants so hired substitutes could not take their place in prison.

In 1880, after Faulds published his paper in *Nature,* Herschel retorted with a claim that he had been using fingerprints as a means to identify criminals in jails since 1860. Herschel published his opinion in a November 1880 article titled "Skin Furrows of the Hand," which was also published in *Nature* magazine. Herschel, however, had been using fingerprints in bar code form and failed to mention the potential for scientific and forensic use. This battle of letters between Faulds and Herschel lasted until 1917, when Herschel finally conceded that Faulds had been the first person to suggest in public a forensic use of fingerprints. Herschel died in 1918, shortly after admitting that Faulds was indeed the first to discover fingerprints' potential use for identification. Although Herschel was not the first to mention publicly the usefulness of fingerprints, he was one of the first to recognize their value.

## ALPHONSE BERTILLON AND THE TRANSITION TO DACTYLOGRAPHY

Perhaps one of the most influential people when speaking of criminal identification, is Alphonse Bertillon. He was born in 1853 to a family with strong scientific traditions. His grandfather was a well-known naturalist and mathematician, and he was the son of a distinguished French physician and statistician. Ironically, Bertillon was a very poor student. He was expelled from several schools and dismissed from an apprenticeship. In 1879 he was able to land a menial job filing information cards on criminals for the Paris police. It was from Bertillon's frustration from these cards that he became noted as the Father of Criminal Identification. Bertillon described the cards as vague, with descriptions that could fit anyone. It was his enthusiasm and curiosity that drove him to compare photographs and take measurements of criminals arrested.

Bertillon concluded that if 11 physical measurements (height, length of outside, length of trunk, head length, head width, cheek width, length of right ear, length of left foot, length of left middle finger, length of left pinkie finger, and length of forearm) of a person were taken, the chances of finding another person with the same 11 measurements were 4,191,304 to 1. He called his system of measurements "anthropometry." Bertillon stored the measurements on a card, which yielded one of the problems of anthropometry—no readily searchable system.

Bertillon's anthropometrical system of personal identification was divided into three integrated parts: (1) the bodily measurements that required measurements, conducted under carefully prescribed conditions on a series of the most characteristic dimensions of bony parts of the human anatomy; (2) the morphological description of the appearance and shape of the body and its measured parts as they related to movements "and even the most characteristic mental and moral qualities"; and (3) a description of "peculiar marks" observed on the surface of the body, resulting from disease, accident, deformity, or artificial disfigurement, such as moles, warts, scars, tattoos, and so on.

In 1883 Bertillon's system of anthropometry received worldwide attention when it was implemented in France, on an experimental basis. Bertillon's anthropometric system proved to the world that there was a more reliable way to document criminals. Shortly after the system's release, he identified his first habitual criminal. In 1888 Bertillon added another innovation to his system, the *portrait parlé*, or "spoken picture." Bertillon's additions of the full-face and profile photographs of each criminal were the predecessors of the modern-day mug shot. Although Bertillon made great strides, many countries abandoned his system of anthropometry after the turn of the century. By the early 20th century, with Fauld's and Herschel's research on dactylography, many countries were turning away from anthropometry. It was because of this that Bertillon reluctantly added fingerprints to his portrait parle. As stated earlier, one of the problems with anthropometry was the need to store filing cards.

After time Bertillon's system became difficult to manage, and that was one of the problems that many countries using anthropometry cited. In 1902 Bertillon solved the murder of Joseph Riebel, when he discovered the fingerprint of Henri Scheffer on the pane of a glass cupboard. His primary focus in this case was how to photograph the fingerprint without destroying the evidence. Bertillon's work in criminal identification helped him pioneer the use of photography to enhance fingerprints. It was this specific case that not only underscored the practical use of photography in criminal investigation but also illustrated the value of dactylography.

The downfall of Bertillon's system was the Will West case. In 1903 Will West arrived at the U.S. Penitentiary at Leavenworth, Kansas. While West was being processed as a new arrival the penitentiary, an employee recognized him. There was already a photograph and Bertillon measurements for Will West, the employee said. A comparison of fingerprints of this new arrival with the information on file revealed that despite almost identical appearances, the identification card belonged to William West, an inmate who had been at Leavenworth since 1901. According to prison records via family correspondence, the two Wests were actually twin brothers. The West cases finalized dactylography's superiority to anthropometry. Although the West case proved that Bertillon's system was imperfect, it served the field of criminal identification for some 10 years. Bertillon died in 1914, leaving behind a legacy of hard work and dedication.

## SIR FRANCIS GALTON'S FINGERPRINT SYSTEM

Sir Francis Galton was born on February 16, 1822, in Sparkbroom, England. A Renaissance man, he is considered one of the greatest scientists of the 19th century. Prior to getting involved in criminology, Galton studied finance, meteorology, psychology, and heredity at Birmingham,

London, and Cambridge. He left school and traveled to Africa in the hope of studying geography. Galton reviewed Bertillon's anthropometric system, as well as dactylography, and supported fingerprinting as the superior method of criminal identification. He also contacted Faulds and Herschel in attempts to study their work. Herschel unselfishly turned over his research, hoping that Galton's interest would revive the practical use of fingerprints.

Galton's primary interest in fingerprints was as an aid in determining heredity and racial background. He soon discovered that fingerprints offered no firm clues to an individual's intelligence or genetic history:

> The races I have chiefly examined are English, most of whom are
> the upper and middle classes; the others chiefly from London board
> schools; Welsh, from the purest Welsh-speaking districts of South
> Wales; Jews from the large London schools, and Negroes from the ter-
> ritories of the Royal Niger Company. I have also a collection of Basque
> prints taken at Cambo, some twenty miles inland from Biarritz, which,
> although small, is large enough to warrant a provisional conclusion.
> As a first and only an approximately correct description, the English,
> Welsh, Jews, Negroes, and Basques, may all be spoken of as identical in
> the character of their finger prints; the same familiar patterns appear-
> ing in all of them which much the same degrees of frequency, the dif-
> ferences between groups of different races being not larger than those
> that occasionally occur between groups of the same race.

He was, however, able to scientifically prove what Herschel and Faulds already suspected: Fingerprints do not change over the course of an individual's lifetime, and no two fingerprints are exactly the same. According to his calculations, the odds of two individual fingerprints

Arch, loop, and whorl *(Courtesy of the author)*

being the same were one in 64 billion. Galton published these findings in his 1892 book *Finger Prints* that presented this statistical proof of the uniqueness of fingerprints and outlined many other principles of identification by fingerprints.

Galton has been noted as the inventor of dermatographics (fingerprint identification) because he was the first to place their study on a scientific basis, and this accomplishment laid the groundwork for their use in criminal cases. Galton was responsible for the basic nomenclature still used today: *arch, loop,* and *whorl.* In 1909 Galton was knighted for his numerous contributions to the field of criminal identification. He died in 1911.

## JUAN VUCETICH'S FINGERPRINT SYSTEM

Ivan Vučetić was born in Croatia on July 20, 1858. He immigrated to Argentina in 1882, where his name was changed to Juan Vucetich as a method of assimilation. He began working as a supervisor of several sanitation workers for Obras Sanitaria. In 1888 Vucetich began employment with the Central Police Department in Argentina, earning $30 a month.

In 1891 Vucetich began the first fingerprint files based on Galton pattern types. He studied Bertillon's and Galton's work, and during his course of study Vucetich discovered the papillary grooves on fingertips. He recorded that when one touches something, a mark is left via perspiration. Shortly after Vucetich's discovery the Argentine police created an office to identify potential offenders held in their jail. The chief of police of the province of Buenos Aires, Guillermo Nunez, put Vucetich in charge of organizing the Office of Anthropometric Identification. He gave Vucetich the May 2, 1891, issue of *Scientific Review,* which contained an article about digital impressions (that is, marks left by fingers). Nunez told him that he needed to create a system to classify fingerprints. Vucetich accepted this challenge and began a comparative analysis of all the fingerprints that came through their facilities. For the time being, however, the police department decided to include the Bertillon system with the fingerprint files.

Vucetich came up with 101 types of fingerprints, which he classified with the incomplete taxonomy of Galton. Vucetich believed that there were four fundamental forms that repeated themselves in fingerprints, which he classified as A-1, T-2, E-3, and V-4. In August 1891 Vucetich's system was used for the first time to register offenders entering their jail facilities. The next year Vucetich got the opportunity to make his first criminal identification using his fingerprint system. He was able to identify a woman who had murdered her two sons and cut her own throat in an attempt to place blame on another. Her bloody print was left on a doorpost, proving her identity as the murderer. In 1894 Vucetich published *Dactiloscopia Comparada* (Comparative fingerprinting), outlining his method of fingerprint classification.

Vucetich continued to work for the government, studying, researching, and classifying fingerprints using his method. In 1911 the provincial government of Buenos Aires passed a law requiring fingerprint registration for all adults subject to military service and who were eligible to vote. Vucetich completed this task by 1913 and decided to take some time away from work and travel. Upon his return to Argentina Vucetich faced humiliation. Although Buenos Aires decided to expand the fingerprint registration laws, the government faced strong protests. By 1917 the government canceled registrations, seized Vucetich's records, and forbade him to continue his work. In 1925 Vucetich died a disappointed man. Although Vucetich's system is still used in Argentina and many other Spanish-speaking countries today, he was never able to see how his classification system benefited the world.

## SIR EDWARD HENRY'S SYSTEM: THE DAWN OF MODERN FINGERPRINT IDENTIFICATION

Perhaps one of the most influential people involved with the evolution of fingerprinting is Sir Edward Henry. Born on July 26, 1850, in London, Henry studied English, Latin, physics, and mathematics at St. Edmund's College and University College. In 1873 Henry qualified for the Indian Civil Service and was appointed to the presidency of Fort William in Bengal, India.

In October 1873 Henry was appointed assistant magistrate collector for the government of the Northwest Provinces. His duties were to preside over the court where tax claims and disputes were adjudicated. In 1891 Henry was appointed to the office of inspector general of the Bengal Police Department. It was during this time that Henry developed an interest in fingerprinting. Henry and Galton began exchanging letters and discussed the merits of fingerprinting. In 1892 the Bengal police force adopted Bertillon's anthropometric system to identify criminals, adding fingerprints to the cards. In 1893 Henry obtained a copy of Galton's book, *Finger Prints,* and began composing a simple yet reliable way to classify fingerprints.

Henry's classification system was completed in February 1897. This system assigned numerical values to each digit, starting with the right thumb (designated 1) through to the left little finger (designated 10). This standard notation is printed on all fingerprint record cards in those countries that use Henry's system. The numbered digits are often considered in pairs, written in the form of a fraction, which is given an arbitrary numerical value.

In March 1897 a commission was set up by British authorities to examine Bertillon's anthropometric system and Henry's classification system. A unanimous verdict established Henry's system as the accepted method for identifying criminals. Six months later it was adopted throughout British India, and in 1900 England began using it. Henry published *Classification and Use of Finger Prints* in 1901, explaining his system and its superiority to anthropometry. That same year Henry was appointed assistant police commissioner of London.

During his appointment the first fingerprint bureau was established at Scotland Yard. He rose to the post of commissioner of Scotland Yard two years later and was knighted in 1906. Ironically, Henry was the victim of an attempted murder. In 1912 he was on the doorsteps to his Kensington house, and someone fired three shots at him. One bullet struck Henry, but he survived the attack. In August 1918 the Metropolitan and City of London Police Officers went on strike. The strike, which lasted more than 44 hours, prompted Henry to resign as commissioner. Henry died of a heart attack in 1931. He left behind him the establishment of the fingerprint classification system that is most used worldwide.

According to David Ashbaugh, an established expert in the field of dactylography and a member of the Royal Mounted Canadian Police, "The Henry Classification System started what is considered the modern era of finger print identification. The fact that the Henry System is the basis for most of the classification systems presently used today speaks for itself."

The history of the development of fingerprint technology is both interesting and varied. Inquiring minds and necessity combined to develop a new technology that addressed a need that is no less important in modern times. It is somewhat humbling to study the efforts of obviously very intelligent individuals who solved their problems unaided by computers or other modern technology. Equally humbling is the fact that those solutions are still applicable in this modern age.

# 3

# Scientific Principles, Instrumentation, and Equipment

**W**hile basic principles of scientific inquiry have changed little over the last several hundred years, the technology used to assist in those inquiries and to implement the findings have changed significantly and, doubtless, will continue to do so. This section will examine the principles of scientific inquiry and the technology that is relied upon accordingly.

## THE THEORY OF INDIVIDUAL IDENTIFICATION AND THE SCIENTIFIC METHOD

The goal of all physical evidence examinations is to achieve individual identification, that is, to show that a fingerprint came from a particular individual or that a bullet was fired in a certain weapon. Being able to accomplish this requires an organized thought process and the execution of a logical series of tests. The scientific method is used in both of these processes.

The scientific method involves a series of steps that ultimately lead to a conclusion. The steps associated with the scientific method are as follows:

1. Define the problem.

2. Make observations.

3. Form a hypothesis (theory).

4. Carry out tests.

5. Refine the hypothesis as necessary.

6. Develop a theory.

This process of critical thinking is applied to each item of physical evidence in an effort to achieve individual identification. When the scientific method is applied to the identification of bullets, cartridge cases, and other ammunition components the process is known as firearms identification.

## FIREARMS IDENTIFICATION

The field of firearms identification is typically associated with tool mark identification. In reality much of firearms identification entails a specific area of tool mark identification. By definition, a tool mark results from the contact of one surface with another, the harder of which is the tool. Thus, in the case of a firearm and a bullet, the firearm is the tool that produces tool marks on the surface of the bullet as it moves through the barrel upon discharge of the firearm. Likewise, the examination of firing pin impressions, magazine marks, extractor marks, ejector marks, breech face marks, and chamber marks on fired cartridge cases all constitute tool mark examinations.

Firearms identification also involves examinations other than tool marks, and these account for the distinction between the two disciplines. The analysis of gunpowder patterns on clothing, the determination of cartridge case ejection patterns, the measurement of trigger pull, or establishing bullet trajectory are examples of this discipline. Likewise, weapons function testing, shot pellet pattern testing, and serial number restoration are additional non-tool mark comparison aspects of firearms identification.

Firearms identification is often referred to as "forensic ballistics" or simply "ballistics," but this is a misnomer, as ballistics is limited to the study of projectile behavior. Ballistics, in the true sense, includes three

## Applying the Scientific Method

Suppose that a fired cartridge case is found at a crime scene. Also present is a 9 mm pistol. The firearms examiner uses the scientific method to evaluate these items of physical evidence.

Step 1: Define the problem. Was the cartridge case found at the scene fired from the 9 mm pistol?

Step 2: Make observations.

- The fired cartridge case has "9 mm Luger" stamped on the base.

- The weapon is chambered for a 9 mm Luger.

- The weapon is a Glock (manufactured in Austria by Glock Industries).

- Glock 9 mm semiautomatic pistols produce rectangular firing pin impressions in the primers of cartridge cases they fire.

- The cartridge case found at the scene has a clearly recognizable rectangular firing pin impression.

Step 3: Form a hypothesis or theory. The fired cartridge case found at the scene was fired in the Glock pistol also found at the scene.

Step 4: Carry out tests. The fired cartridge case and the Glock pistol are taken back to the crime laboratory, where the pistol is test-fired and the fired cartridge cases produced are compared to the evidence cartridge case using a forensic comparison microscope. The results indicate that the evidence cartridge case has general features like those present on the test fires, but there are marks on the test fires that are not present on the evidence cartridge case and vice versa.

Step 5: Modify the hypothesis. The cartridge case found at the scene was not fired from the pistol also found at the scene. The pistol found at the scene does not appear to have been involved.

Step 6: Develop a theory. A Glock pistol, or a weapon that produces similar marks on cartridge cases, was used to fire the cartridge case found at the scene.

different aspects: interior ballistics (bullet behavior within the confines of the barrel), exterior ballistics (bullet behavior upon exiting the barrel), and terminal ballistics (bullet behavior upon impacting a target). Wound ballistics is a specialized area of terminal ballistics relating to the behavior of bullets striking human or animal targets.

Tool mark examination, on the other hand, is limited to the determination of whether a tool mark was made by a particular tool. Tools commonly examined and compared to questioned (evidence) tool marks include pliers, saws, screw drivers, pry bars, hammers, chisels, and the like.

Tool marks are of two different types: impressed and striated. Impressed tool marks result when a tool leaves an impression, or dent, on another surface. An example would be the result of a blow from a hammer on soft wood. Striated tool marks are the result of a combination of force and motion. The example of a gun barrel producing a tool mark on a bullet illustrates the production of striated tool marks. A cut in metal with a pair of shears is another example. The striations that are produced are often visible only under magnification (with a microscope).

The basis for determining that a particular tool produced a certain tool mark is the presence of random, unique marks that only that tool could have left. In order to be able to properly evaluate firearm and tool mark evidence, an examiner must have extensive training and knowledge about manufacturing techniques of firearms and tools. This is required so that the examiner can distinguish between what are random, unique marks, or "individual characteristics," and what are merely "class characteristics" or "subclass characteristics."

Class characteristics are those characteristics exhibited by an entire group or class of tools. An example would be the width of the blade of a particular brand of screwdriver or the cross-sectional diameter of a gun barrel (caliber) of a certain brand and model firearm.

Subclass characteristics are produced incidental to manufacture and can change over time. Thus, only certain members (a subset) of a class or group will exhibit them. An example would be tools made using a mold or die having some defect that carries over to the tool. Once the die or mold wears such that the defect disappears, or the die or mold is replaced, the subclass characteristic does not appear on subsequently manufactured tools. A group of firearms or ammunition components can also exhibit various properties that are limited to that group and not the entire population at large.

Individual characteristics are unique to a particular tool or firearm to the exclusion of all similar tools or firearms. They are accidental or random characteristics that provide a basis for individualization. Individual characteristic may be produced in manufacture and/or through use (wear). Thus, the interior surfaces of gun barrels exhibit unique characteristics due to manufacture and wear.

The actual comparison and ultimate identification of individual characteristics evaluates quantitative and qualitative aspects of the surface contours. Identification is the result of the examiner determining that "sufficient agreement" exists in the surface contours of a test tool mark and an evidence tool mark.

From a practical standpoint it would not be expected that two tool marks would ever be identical. In their article "Criteria for Identification of Tool Marks," which appeared in *AFTE Journal* in 1998, Jerry Miller and Michael McLean put it like this: "Nothing duplicated in nature has been reportedly found to be exactly the same, and man has not been able to produce things exactly alike."

The Association of Firearm and Tool Mark Examiners allows for "opinions of common origin to be made when the unique surface contours of two tool marks are in sufficient agreement." The definition of *sufficient agreement* varies somewhat depending on who is asked to define it, but it generally involves the examiner having looked at a large number of tool marks, particularly known nonmatches (tool marks known to have been made by different tools).

Studies of the number of consecutive matching striae have been conducted. Former firearm examiners from California Al Biasotti and John Murdock have proposed a "conservative criteria for identification" as follows:

1. In three-dimensional tool marks identification is possible when at least three each or one group of six consecutive matching striae appear in the same relative position in an evidence tool mark compared with a test tool mark.

2. In two-dimensional tool marks identification is possible when at least two groups of at least five each or one group of eight consecutive matching striae are in agreement.

There is ongoing study and debate on this subject. The lack of universally accepted criteria for identification has fostered legal challenges to tool mark identification. The problem of articulating criteria for identification lies in the fact that comparisons must take into account not only the quantitative aspect (number of consecutive matching striae) but also the quality of the match. Exactly how to define *quality of match* is somewhat more difficult than establishing the minimum number of consecutive striae for identification.

In the author's opinion the proof of the scientific validity of tool mark evidence lies in the results of studies of consecutively manufactured tools or firearms. In 1994 the author participated in such a test involving consecutively manufactured pistol barrels. This is because carryover tool marks are not likely to occur in the manufacturing process where the same machine, operator, tool, and/or stock are used to produce items one after another.

Testers obtained a group of consecutively manufactured pistol barrels. The purpose of the test was to see if bullets fired through the barrels could be distinguished from one another and, more important, that the bullets could be identified to the specific barrel that fired them. The bottom line was that the bullets were both distinguishable from one another and identifiable to the barrel that fired them.

After decades of court acceptance the scientific validity of tool mark examination has been challenged since the *Daubert v. Merrell Dow Pharmaceuticals* decision of 1993, based on the lack of clearly articulated criteria for identification. Various studies have been undertaken in an effort to resolve this apparent shortcoming. Further discussion of criteria for identification appears in a following section.

## FIREARMS EXAMINATION EQUIPMENT

The specialized equipment used by firearms examiners includes microscopes, measuring tools, testing tools, and balances. These tools enable the examiner to carry out the various aspects of firearms examination

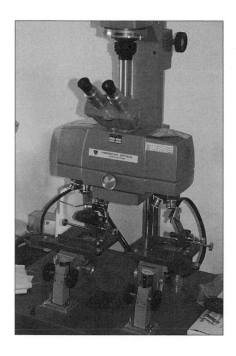

Forensic comparison microscope
*(Courtesy of the author)*

and comparison. The need for proficiency with microscopes empha-
sizes the importance of examiners having an academic background in
science. Other equipment, such as measuring and weighing devices, are
also familiar items to anyone who has a science background.

The firearms or tool marks examiner primarily uses two different
types of microscopes on a regular basis. The first is the stereomicroscope. This microscope sits on the worktable and is usually mounted on
a boom or arm extending from a stand. It usually has zoom capabilities
for magnification from about 3X to about 10X. Initial examinations of
weapons, ammunition components, tools, and objects with tool marks
on them are done with the stereomicroscope. The relatively low power
gives plenty of working room so that the examiner can manipulate various cumbersome objects into the field of view.

The workhorse of the firearms or tool marks section is the forensic
comparison microscope, which is actually two microscopes connected
via an optical bridge. When one looks through the eyepieces, both stages
are visible via a split screen. In this way evidence tool marks on a surface
can be compared directly to test tool marks on a similar surface. The

View through a comparison microscope *(Courtesy of the author)*

photographs show a forensic comparison microscope and a comparison of two bullets where the parallel lines are the microscopic tool marks produced by the interior surfaces of the gun barrel.

Forensic comparison microscopes have special holders that fit on the stages so that a wide variety of evidence items, such as bullets, cartridge cases, shot shells, tools, and firearms and parts, can be examined. The examiner must sometimes improvise in order to get a desired part under the microscope.

Comparison microscopes are fitted with multiple objectives so that a range of magnification is available to the examiner. A maximum of about 40X magnification is typically adequate for firearms or tool marks examination.

The comparison microscope is usually fitted with a video imaging system for use in training and for case documentation purposes. Digital images showing the specific areas of identification provide visual support for the examiner's written notes and conclusions. Not everyone supports the use of photography. Critics argue against photographing

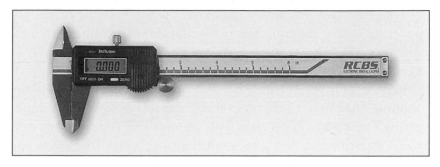

Dial calipers *(Courtesy of the author)*

identifications on the basis that two-dimensional photographs do not fully represent the three-dimensional tool marks.

While there is a measure of truth to this argument, such images are useful for refreshing the examiner's memory of the comparison at a later date and for allowing a defense expert to see the basis for the identification. Of course, some tool marks have no perceptible depth, and thus, the argument is completely lost in those cases.

Firearms and tool marks examiners use a number of different measuring tools in the process of examining evidence. Digital calipers allow accurate measurements of thicknesses and depths to one-thousandth of an inch. Micrometers are also used to measure thicknesses and are accurate to one-thousandth of an inch as well. Such measurements come into play with firearms and ammunition components in particular where various comparisons of size are being made.

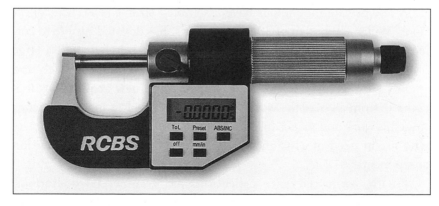

Micrometer *(Courtesy of the author)*

Trigger pull weights, scales, and/or electronic measuring devices are used in the testing and evaluation of functionality of firearms. Extremely light or extremely heavy trigger pulls can be a factor in whether a shooting was intentional or not.

In order to have test bullets for comparison to evidence bullets, the examiner must have a bullet trap that is capable of catching and preserving fired bullets. Water traps typically consist of large stainless steel boxes (approximately $30 \times 48 \times 96$ inches) with a pipe attached to one end to fire into. Filter systems for both the air and the water help keep the working environment safe.

As already discussed in chapter 1, firearms examiners sometimes need example weapons for comparisons or need to have parts available so that an evidence weapon received with a broken part might be test-fired anyway by replacing the part. Reference collections of tools and ammunition are also important. Ammunition of known origin assists the examiner in identifying various ammunition components submitted for examination. Having reference bolt cutters, saws, pliers, screwdrivers, and other tools can provide information as to the presence of class, subclass, and individual characteristics.

Large law-enforcement agencies are one source of such reference collections. The NYPD Crime Laboratory, in addition to having a large firearms reference collection, has some weapons of historical significance. The revolver used by the serial killer known as the "Son of Sam" (David Berkowitz) and the weapon used to murder former Beatle John Lennon are among the weapons in their gun vault.

A few private individuals have assembled sizable reference collections. William Wooden of Tucson, Arizona, has devoted his life to collecting and cataloging ammunition components. He has built a large underground bunker on his property to house his collection safely and spends most of his waking hours working with new acquisitions that come in from all over the world. He has established an institute to continue his work and makes his resources available to firearms examiners who are in need of assistance with the identification of ammunition components.

Finally, some reference collections are commercial operations. George Kass of Michigan operates Forensic Ammunition Service, a business that provides police agencies with exemplars of unusual and rare ammunition. His inventory is constantly growing and includes ammunition from both foreign and domestic sources. Although there is a fee for ammunition requested from Forensic Ammunition Service, it is modest.

## SPECIALIZED EQUIPMENT FOR SHOOTING RECONSTRUCTION

The reconstruction of a shooting incident is the most challenging part of a firearms examiner's job. This is the culmination of all the scientific and criminal investigations relating to a particular incident wherein a theory for the shooting is postulated. Unless such a theory can be developed, the individual firearms examination results are often inadequate in and of themselves to explain the shooting circumstances to a jury in a criminal proceeding. Shooting reconstruction requires specialized knowledge and equipment beyond that of the typical firearms examiner. This means specialized training and significant field experience are necessary for a firearms examiner to be qualified to reconstruct shooting incidents.

There are special considerations involved in the reconstruction of shooting incidents. For example, examiners may want to estimate the shooter's position. As a result, there are special needs in terms of equipment. For starters, trajectory rods are inserted into bullet holes to determine bullet trajectories. An angle gauge is used to determine angles of impact into vertical surfaces. A laser attached to the end of a trajectory rod allows the trajectory rod to be "extended" out great distances. The first photograph shows the basic kit, which includes rods, angle gauge, tripod mount, and centering cones.

The second photograph shows a trajectory rod inserted into a bullet hole through a portion of a solid core door. The laser has been attached to the end of the rod and the angle gauge has been put in place. In this way the investigator is able to establish the paths of bullets at crime scenes and ultimately determine the probable position of the shooter. By taking angle measurements the investigator can create a scale diagram to assist the jury in understanding the circumstances of the shooting.

It is easy to determine vertical angles using an angle gauge, but what about the side-to-side angle that must also be measured? There will be both a vertical angle and a horizontal angle of impact, as shown in the diagram. Both of these angles need to be determined to create a scale diagram.

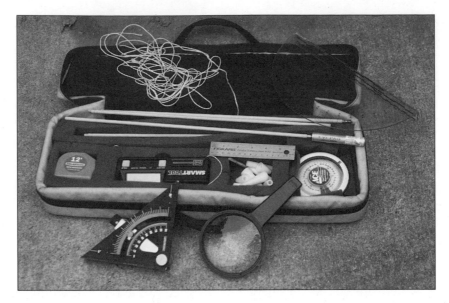

Trajectory kit *(Courtesy of the author)*

Trajectory rod, angle gauge, and laser *(Courtesy of the author)*

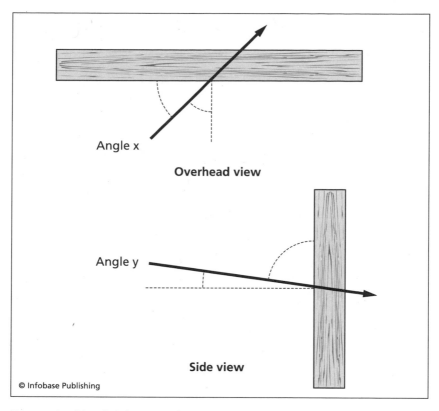

Two angles (*X* and *Y*) that must be measured in trajectory analysis

To measure a nonvertical angle, a protractor is required because the angle gauge only works in the vertical, or *Y*, direction. Angles in the horizontal, or *X*, direction can only be measured using a protractor. Not just any old protractor will work, however. The protractor must be such that the base is the point of origin (that is, has a value of zero degrees). This requires what is known as a zero-base protractor. A zero-base protractor is shown in the photograph.

The zero-base protractor may be used to measure both angles in trajectory analysis. However, when measuring the vertical (*Y*) angle of a trajectory rod on an uneven surface, such as a car side panel, it is necessary to use a standard plane of reference, such as a plane perpendicular to the ground. This is particularly important when there are multiple bullet holes that require trajectory analysis. If there is no common or standard plane of reference, the angles recorded have no meaning. The method used to overcome this dilemma is to hold a plumb bob (conical

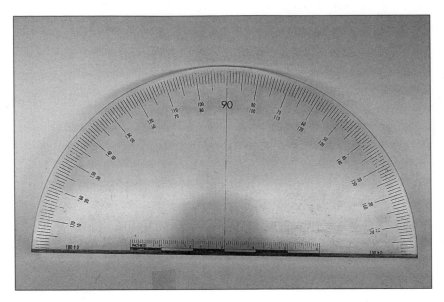

Zero-base protractor *(Courtesy of the author)*

metal weight) on a string out some distance from the surface. The zero-base protractor is then held parallel to the plumb line that represents a perpendicular plane, as illustrated in the photograph.

When the bullet hole being examined is in a thin material, such as thin, aluminum siding, it is not possible to use a trajectory rod to determine the angles. This is because the trajectory rod must have two surfaces, one in front and one in back, with at least an inch of separation to rest on in order to demonstrate the bullet trajectory. When the bullet-damaged material is too thin, a laser protractor is used in a process that involves measuring the bullet hole and calculating the angle of impact. The examiner then sets this angle on the protractor, making the laser project the trajectory.

Additional equipment may be required to reconstruct a shooting incident, and this varies depending on the particular circumstances of the shooting. For instance, the firearms examiner will often need to test the angle at which it appears that a bullet struck a particular target (any inanimate object). To do this a fixture with a rotating target holder is used. This allows the angle of the gun barrel to the target to be set precisely. It is much simpler to rotate the target and keep the weapon fixed in position than it is to try to position the weapon at a particular angle.

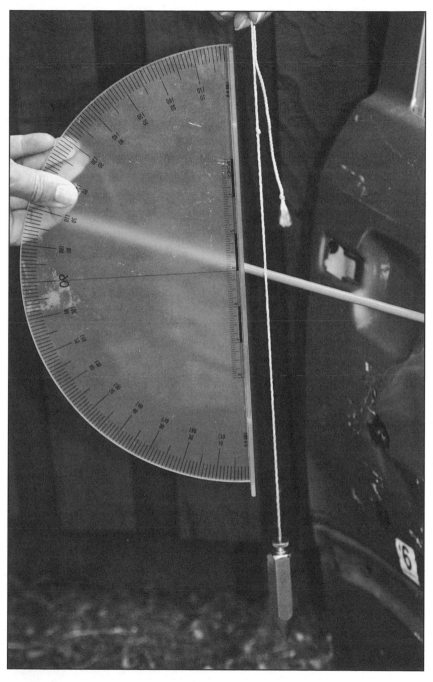

Plumb bob and zero-base protractor *(Courtesy of the author)*

Laser protractor *(Courtesy of the author)*

Angle-of-impact determination
fixture *(Courtesy of the author)*

The fixture shown in the photograph is made up by the examiner and illustrates the fact that not all the needed equipment is available commercially. Thus, the examiner must be somewhat mechanically inclined and have good problem-solving skills in addition to the academic and training requirements already cited.

## LABORATORY METHODS FOR FIREARMS EVIDENCE

There are a number of questions regarding firearms and ammunition components that the firearms examiner can potentially answer.

- Is the gun operable?

- Has the gun been damaged or modified?

- Is there evidence of recent firing on or in the gun?

- Did the gun fire the ammunition components (cartridge case or bullet) that were also submitted with it?

- How far from the target was the gun when it was fired?

Operability testing begins with a visual inspection of the weapon and hand cycling of the action. For a revolver this means cocking the hammer and pulling the trigger to see if the weapon appears to be functioning properly. If the weapon is double action (that is, pulling the trigger both cocks the hammer and fires the weapon), the examiner pulls the trigger while observing the cylinder to see that it rotates. The hammer is also observed to see that it cocks.

It is also possible to insert a wooden dowel rod into the barrel with one end against the firing pin opening. With the barrel pointed straight up to keep the dowel rod against the firing pin opening in the breech face, the trigger is pulled. If the firing pin is functioning properly, the rod can be observed to rise upon impact by the firing pin. The idea is that if there is enough impact force to visibly move the dowel rod, then a cartridge could be fired. This method allows the examiner to determine quickly operability without having to fire a weapon. It also saves expenses on ammunition and lessens the examiner's exposure to noise and vaporous residues.

For semiautomatic weapons operability questions include whether the weapon will eject fired cartridge cases and reload as designed by the manufacturer. For this testing the weapon must actually be fired. From a purely legal standpoint, however, it is only necessary that a weapon be capable of firing a single round in order for it to qualify as a firearm.

If a weapon appears to be potentially unsafe, the examiner can set it up in a fixture that will hold it securely. The examiner then ties a string to the trigger and stands behind a protective barrier so that the weapon

## Firearms Testing: Sympathetic Firing

A homicide victim was found to have two bullet wounds at autopsy. The suspect's weapon was a small, cheaply made 22-caliber revolver. Inspection of the contents of the revolver cylinder indicated that there were two fired cartridge cases. However, the location of the two fired cartridge cases was out of sequence. The cylinder rotated clockwise as the weapon was fired, but there was a fired cartridge case under the hammer and a second fired cartridge case two spaces counterclockwise from the first.

When the firearms examiner inspected the bullets recovered from the victim's body at autopsy, he noted that one of the two bullets was devoid of rifling marks. He also noted that the autopsy report described one of the entry wounds as being "irregular" and "suggestive of having struck an intermediate target." An inspection of the fired cartridge cases told the story of what had happened. The cartridge case that appeared out of sequence relative to the one found under the hammer had an uncharacteristic indentation in the rim: It did not have a firing pin impression consistent with this weapon. Examination of the revolver revealed that the cylinder was loose in the frame of the revolver and was capable of sliding back and forth approximately 3 mm.

Under interrogation the suspect finally admitted to having fired one round at the decedent. Although participants often cannot accurately remember the actual number of shots fired in a shooting incident, in may be safely fired by pulling the string from a distance. Revolvers with loose and/or misaligned cylinders are common examples of potentially dangerous weapons. Weapons are never loaded with more than one round, for safety purposes.

The examination of firearms to determine whether they have been damaged or modified is a direct spin-off of the function and reliability testing. This phase of the examination for semiautomatic weapons, however, often focuses on whether the weapon has been modified to be fully automatic (that is, once the trigger is pulled, the weapon continues

this case the firearms examiner had multiple clues as to what had taken place: sympathetic firing. Sympathetic firing is firing that occurs when the cylinder moves backward as it is fired, causing a second round to contact the frame and discharge. The bullet exits the chamber without ever entering the barrel, thus, no rifling marks are produced. Since the bullet is not spin-stabilized, it begins to tumble in flight, producing an irregular-shaped entry into whatever it strikes.

In order to verify this the firearms examiner had to load multiple rounds in the revolver, set it up in a machine rest, and fire it from a remote location. This precaution was necessary due to the inherently unsafe aspect of firing the weapon while holding it in the hand. Multiple attempts were necessary before sympathetic firing was actually achieved. Given the various indicators present—no rifling marks on the bullet, an inconsistent firing pin impression, out-of-sequence cartridge case location, irregular entry wound, and a loose cylinder—it would not have been absolutely necessary to duplicate the event by testing. The examiner could have simply determined that the weapon would fire, noted all the inconsistencies, and opined that sympathetic firing had taken place. Actually confirming that the weapon would produce sympathetic firing was, of course, the most scientifically sound course of action.

to fire until the magazine is empty). Fully automatic weapons typically fire more rapidly than semiautomatic weapons. It is a federal offense to make such modifications without having the appropriate federal firearms license. The examiner can test if this modification has occurred by pulling the trigger, holding it back, and cycling the action. In a weapon that will reliably fire fully automatic, the hammer should fall each time the action is manually cycled. If instead the trigger must be released and then pulled to make the hammer fall, this test confirms the gun to be semiautomatic only.

## Identifying the Use of a Sound Suppressor

A quadruple homicide occurred in northeast Texas in the late 1990s. Each of the four victims was shot in the back of the head two or three times. The bullets, recovered at autopsy, were all 22 caliber and were determined to have all been fired by the same weapon. The shootings took place inside an establishment that was part of a business park with adjoining businesses on either side separated by sheetrock walls. No one on either side reported hearing gunshots even though a total of 10 shots were fired and the shooting took place during regular business hours.

Upon examination of the recovered bullets the firearms examiner noted the same type of shaved area on the side of each bullet. From that he concluded that a sound suppressor may have been present on the weapon.

Ultimately, authorities determined that a disgruntled customer of the business had been there on the day of the murders but had lied when first questioned about it. A search warrant of the individual's residence was obtained that specified confiscation of any weapons, ammunition, suppressors, or related materials.

Although no weapons or ammunition were found during the search, searchers did find a receipt for a Ruger Mark II 22-caliber semiautomatic pistol. Another receipt was found indicating an earlier order for a case of Fiocchi (an Italian ammunition manufacturer) 22-caliber subsonic

Sometimes the "backyard gunsmith" does not fully accomplish his goal of converting a semiautomatic weapon to fully automatic, resulting in a weapon that will occasionally fire in the fully automatic mode. Actual test-firing is often the only way to confirm this. The firearms examiner can load two or three rounds initially and attempt to get the weapon to fire multiple rounds with one pull of the trigger. If this is unsuccessful, a full magazine may be used. By examining the internal workings of the weapon the examiner can usually tell if there has been any attempt made to modify the weapon. Directions

ammunition. According to records of the supplier, the suspect had received the ammunition several months prior to the murders. Perhaps most incriminating was an instruction sheet for a suppressor tube from a firearms accessory company.

The firearms examiner confirmed that in addition to the common shaved areas on the sides of each bullet were rifling marks consistent with a Ruger Mark II pistol. This did not mean that only a Ruger Mark II could have fired the bullets, but it did mean that a Ruger Mark II was among the possible weapons that could have fired them.

Based on his lying to investigators about being at the business the day of the shootings, his acknowledged dispute with the owner, and the circumstantial evidence to support that he acquired subsonic ammunition, a suppressor tube, and a Ruger 22 Mark II pistol, the man was convicted of first-degree murder. At trial his defense had pointed out that subsonic ammunition is available to anyone and is used for target shooting. Likewise, the Ruger Mark II pistol in 22-caliber is a common target pistol. With regard to the suppressor tube brochure it also included other products unrelated to suppressor manufacture. Furthermore, no confirmation of the defendant having ever actually purchased a suppressor or a suppressor tube was ever found. Obviously, the jury did not think there was reasonable doubt about it. What do you think?

for converting various weapons to fire fully automatic are available on the Internet.

Another modification that the firearms examiner may encounter is a sound suppressor. These are generally referred to as "silencers," although that is a misnomer. The only way to completely silence a firearm is not to fire it. Sound suppressors are only feasible with single shot, semiautomatic, or fully automatic weapons. Revolvers cannot be effectively suppressed due to the open space between the cylinder and the frame. The sources of sound involved in the discharge of a weapon are the expansion of hot gases from the powder and primer, the bullet breaking the sound barrier, and the action of the weapon (the hammer falling and slide moving back to reload). The latter two are most easily taken care of. The use of subsonic ammunition, that is bullets traveling slower than the speed of sound, eliminates the sonic boom associated with a supersonic bullet as it breaks the sound barrier. The action of the weapon can be locked so that it does not cycle.

The expanding hot gases create most of the noise associated with the discharge of a firearm. By slowing down the rate of expansion, the sound may be suppressed. Devices used for this purpose range from a two-liter plastic bottle placed over the gun muzzle to sophisticated metal expansion chambers containing baffles of various types and designs. These more sophisticated suppressors may be integral to the barrel or screw onto the end of the barrel.

In any event all that is required for there to be a violation of the National Firearms Act is for there to be any decrease in the audible report of the weapon. This may simply be determined by the examiner test-firing the weapon in question with and without the alleged suppressor and listening for a discernable decrease in the report. A more reliable method is to used a decibel meter to record the number of decibels produced with and without the device. This allows the examiner to establish a quantitative measure of the sound suppression. Again, even the slightest decrease in the audible sound constitutes a violation of federal law if the device has not been registered with the ATF. Thus, an aluminum soda can or a plastic bottle would conceivably have to be registered as a suppressor to be legally placed over the muzzle of a firearm.

The question of whether there is evidence of a weapon being fired can be answered conclusively in some instances. Many times the results of these examinations are inconclusive. The amount of time that has passed since the time of the shooting is a primary consideration. For example, if a shooting took place only a matter of hours or even days before and a suspect weapon is determined to have a barrel that is full of dust, corrosion, or other foreign material, it is extremely unlikely that the weapon was used in the shooting.

On the other hand, a thoroughly clean barrel cannot be taken as evidence of anything other than that the owner is meticulous about his or her weapon. Even finding a few gunpowder particles inside the barrel only allows an examiner to be able to say that there is evidence of firing since the last time the weapon was cleaned. In most instances there would be no way to conclusively determine when that time of last cleaning was.

When a revolver is fired, a pattern of soot is deposited around the margins of the chamber on the face of the revolver cylinder. The term *halo* or *cylinder flare* is used to identify these deposits, as shown in the photograph. This soot pattern can be correlated with the rotation direction of the cylinder, the chamber under the hammer, and the number of fired cartridge cases to help establish evidence of recent firing. For example, if only one shot was fired in a shooting incident and a revolver is suspected to be the responsible weapon, the presence of a single cylinder flare would be circumstantial evidence that this could be the responsible weapon.

Research is currently being done to use the vaporous residue present in gun barrels and fired cartridge cases to establish approximate time since firing. These residues persist for up to a day or longer, then totally dissipate. By determining the presence and quantity of these residues, researchers hope to be able to estimate reliably the time of shooting. This work may lead to a method that can be used to confirm what presently can only be speculated.

As has been previously described, the firearms examiner's most common task is to determine whether bullets, cartridge cases, and shot shells have been fired in weapons either found at crime scenes or recovered from suspects. To do this the firearms examiner must obtain ammunition similar to that in question. The reason for this is that differences in the hardness of bullets and cartridge case brass can result in differences in the markings left by firearms. For example, lead bullets and copper jacketed bullets (that is, bullets consisting of an inner core of lead with

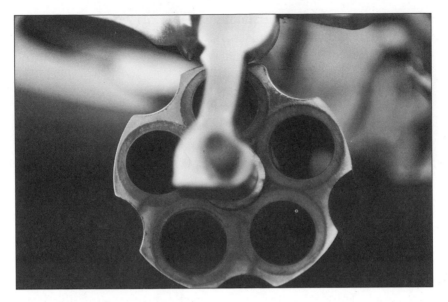

Cylinder flare *(Courtesy of the author)*

an outer skin of copper) acquire significantly different markings. Primer case composition can also vary, and some primer cases are much harder than others. This can also result in significantly different marks from the same firing pins and breech faces. As in any scientifically based test, the examiner must duplicate the actual event as closely as possible in order to be able to produce any meaningful results.

The firearms examiner will typically fire a minimum of three test rounds from the suspect weapon. The water trap is used to stop the bullets and minimize their distortion and alteration of surface markings from the interior of the gun barrel. Even with water, however, high-velocity bullets can distort and even disintegrate upon impact with the surface. Anyone who has done a belly flop into water knows that water is really not that soft! The firearms examiner must sometimes reduce the powder charge in a cartridge in order to slow the bullet enough to keep it from distorting or disintegrating. To do this the examiner refers to charts found in reloading manuals for "reduced loads" and manually reduces the powder charge of a commercially produced cartridge.

First the examiner removes the bullet using a tool known as an inertia bullet puller. This resembles a plastic mallet with a hollow head. The

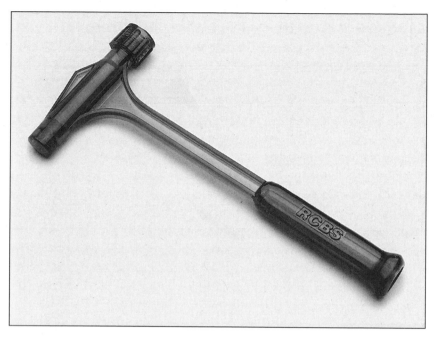

Bullet puller *(Courtesy of the author)\*

cartridge is placed into a special collet (holder) that holds it in the hollow space. The puller is then struck against a hard surface with a swinging motion, like one would strike a blow with a hammer. The inertia of the bullet causes it to dislodge from the case while the collet holds the cartridge case in place. The examiner removes the powder, weights out a lesser portion, places it back into the cartridge case, then manually reinserts the bullet into the cartridge case. The reduced load is now ready to be fired.

A potential problem with firing reduced loads is that the cartridge case may not receive markings from the chamber, breech face, and firing pin that are as prominent as those from a full powder charge. This is because less powder results in less force of expansion. With lead bullets, however, less powder can actually result in better retention of barrel markings, since the hot gases associated with a full powder charge have a tendency to erode the soft lead. Copper jacketed bullets do not exhibit this effect.

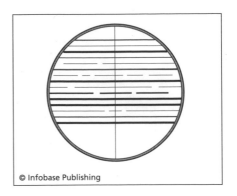

Diagram of striations as viewed
through a microscope

© Infobase Publishing

Once the examiner has collected the fired bullets and cartridge cases, the task of comparing microscopic markings on bullets and cartridge cases begins. This involves mounting two bullets or two cartridge cases on the comparison microscope, one on each side or stage, and carefully observing as one is slowly rotated while the other remains fixed. The idea is to find that particular area where the microscopic markings are of sufficient quality and quantity to call it a match. The figure illustrates the type of markings that the examiner looks for.

To answer the last of the questions posed in this section, the muzzle-to-target distance in a shooting incident, the firearms examiner may use several different approaches depending on the type of weapon involved. For shots from any type weapon the firearms examiner will first look for the presence of gunpowder particles on skin and/or clothing. The general rule of thumb is that gunpowder will be expected to strike the target if the shot was fired within arm's length or less. When a firearm is discharged, gunpowder particles exit the muzzle in a conical distribution. The farther away the target is from the muzzle of the gun, the greater the gunpowder pattern diameter will be, as illustrated in the diagram.

Exactly how far the gunpowder particle will travel horizontally depends on three things: particle shape, gravity, and air friction. Gunpowder for handguns comes in three different shapes known as ball, flattened ball, and flake or disk. To determine which gunpowder particle shape would travel the farthest, given the same initial velocity, one need only imagine trying to throw a soccer ball versus trying to throw a dish or plate baseball style. The aerodynamic shape of the ball powder (spherical) allows it to easily outdistance the other shapes.

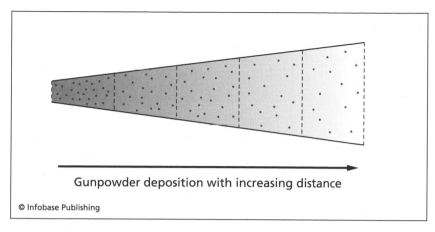

Gunpowder deposition with increasing distance

© Infobase Publishing

Conical distribution of gunpowder particles

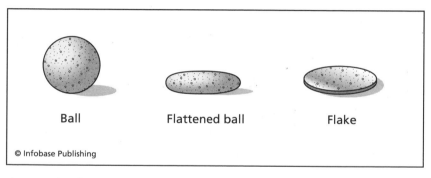

Ball              Flattened ball              Flake

© Infobase Publishing

Gunpowder shapes (as emitted from a handgun)

Like that for handguns, gunpowder designed for use in rifle cartridges also comes in ball, flattened ball, and flake or disk, but tubular powder particles are available as well. The reason for the different powder particle shapes, or morphologies, has to do with differences in burning rates. Gunpowder may consist of nitrocellulose or a combination of nitrocellulose and nitroglycerin (so-called single-base and double-base powder). There is actually quite a lot of physics involved in the design of a cartridge. The reason is the differences in ballistic requirements: different barrel lengths, calibers, bullet weights, and bullet designs require specific loads for optimum performance. Shotgun shells (shot shells) involve similar considerations.

In order to be sure that cartridges can be successfully and safely fired from all sorts of different weapons under a wide variety of atmospheric conditions, manufacturers put more than enough powder in

## Ball Powder Goes the Distance

The ability of ball powder to outdistance other gunpowder shapes is not only a consideration for powder particles traveling through the air but also through bodies and other dense material. In his textbook *Gunshot Wound,* Vincent Dimaio notes that he has encountered cases in which victims were shot through the head at contact or near contact range, and ball powder actually passed through the skull with the bullet.

In another case familiar to this author, a very obese man was shot in the side at contact range with a 357 magnum loaded with ammunition containing ball powder. The bullet exited the man's body on the opposite side. An examination of the man's wound at autopsy revealed gunpowder particles inside the wound tract. Examination of the man's shirt revealed no gunpowder around the entrance hole but a considerable amount of gunpowder on the inside of the shirt around the exit hole. The ball powder had traveled completely through this large man's body!

The author examined a case involving an errant shot in a drive-by shooting that struck and killed a young girl who happened to be standing in the wrong place at the wrong time. Who fired the fatal shot was in dispute. The bullet passed through the victim and was never recovered, so there was no way to identify the shooter's gun. Because two particles of ball powder were found on her clothing, it was proposed that the shot had to come from the man standing in the yard within eight feet (2.4 m) of her and not from the individual who was firing from the vehicle approximately 15 feet (4.6 m) away. An unrelated study conducted by Dimaio, however, showed that individual particles of ball powder fired from a 38-caliber revolver could travel as far as 20 feet (6.1 m). Thus, the shot could have come from the vehicle. Since no one knew which way the little girl had been facing when she was shot and both shooters were firing 38 revolvers with ball powder, it was not possible to rule out either.

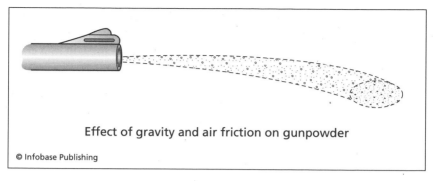

Effect of gravity and air friction on gunpowder

© Infobase Publishing

Ultimate fate of gunpowder particles in flight

their cartridges. This pretty well ensures the fact that unburned and partially burned gunpowder particles will exit the barrel of a weapon when fired.

Regardless of how much or what type of gunpowder is involved, the force of gravity and the effect of air friction both act to slow and eventually bring the powder particles to a halt. Thus, if a weapon is held parallel to the ground and fired, the powder will only go a limited distance before it lands on the ground. Exactly how far this distance might be depends, once again, on things like barrel length and cartridge composition (shape and amount of powder and bullet weight).

In attempting to determine the approximate muzzle-to-target distance, the firearms examiner may also use the behavior of soot and vaporous lead (coming mostly from the lead azide primer). These materials tend to be deposited at very close distances, less than about a foot. When the deposits are present, the examiner can often further define the estimated distance.

The whole process begins with visual and microscopic examination (by stereoscope) to locate the powder particles, followed by chemical testing for lead and nitrites using the sodium rhodizonate test and the Griess test, respectively. Nitrites are the product of the combustion of nitrates, the chemical entity of gunpowder. Once a pattern of nitrites and/or confirmation of vaporous lead has been established, the firearms examiner then carries out a series of test firings using the weapon and ammunition like that used in the shooting. When a similar pattern has been produced and is found to be reproducible, the firearms examiner is able to propose an approximate muzzle-to-target distance.

In the case of a shotgun firing shot, the diameter or density of the shot pattern produced can also be used to help establish distance. Just as gunpowder particles, steel, or lead shot exiting the muzzle of a shotgun travels in a conical distribution, the base diameter of the pattern becomes greater the farther from the muzzle it is. Also like gunpowder particles, the shot is acted upon by the effects of gravity and air friction, which tend to bring the shot pellets to the ground. A rough approximation that works best with buckshot loads is that for each inch of shot pattern diameter, one has another yard of muzzle to target distance. To record the shot pattern a firearms examiner draws a circle that includes all of the shot holes, then uses the diameter of the circle to approximate the distance between the muzzle and the target, as illustrated in the diagram. The results are then confirmed through test firing.

## AUTOMATED COMPARISON OF FIREARMS EVIDENCE

In large police agencies such as the Los Angeles Police Department (LAPD) or the NYPD, a huge number of firearms are confiscated from criminals each year. These guns must necessarily all be test-fired and the test-fired bullets and cartridge cases compared to bullets and cartridge

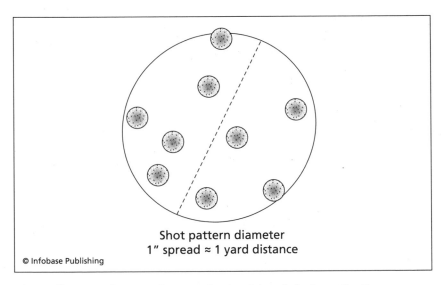

Shot pattern diameter
1″ spread ≈ 1 yard distance

© Infobase Publishing

Shot pellet spread versus distance. A rule of thumb for investigative purposes only.

cases in unsolved cases. This would be an overwhelming task were it not for the advent of computer-based screening. In July 1992 the FBI developed a computer system called Drugfire for comparing the surfaces of fired bullets. The bureau also developed a system for examining the marks left on the bases of cartridge cases called Brass Catcher. In a classic example of bureaucratic duplication of effort, the ATF developed its own system, called Integrated Bullet Identification System (IBIS). Ironically, the two systems could not "talk" to each other because their software was incompatible. At the urging of groups such as the American Society of Crime Laboratory Directors, this problem was resolved, and the ATF system was universally adopted under the name National Integrated Bullet Identification Network (NIBIN). The system allows law-enforcement agencies access to databases in surrounding areas. Unfortunately it does not allow access to every police agency's database. At the NYPD, for example, the system does not currently allow access

## The Community Gun

Prior to the advent of databases of firearms component markings, it was generally believed that individual firearms were used by many different persons to commit crimes, especially in street gangs, but this theory could not be proved because law-enforcement agencies were unable to exchange firearms evidence in a systematic way. Following the introduction of databases for bullet rifling, cartridge case and firing pin impressions, and breech face marks, all that changed.

The FBI, for instance, found that one particular Berretta 9 mm pistol was responsible for two murders in Washington, D.C., a shooting in Baltimore, Maryland, and a holdup in Richmond, Virginia. Different individuals were responsible for each of the crimes, but all were members of the Crips street gang in Washington, D.C. As the months wore on, additional similar links between shooting crimes across wide areas and an individual firearm were found. The FBI was thus able to confirm that street gangs had weapons caches that were available to and used by members.

to the databases of nearby New Jersey. This situation will no doubt be slowly resolved across the country.

Ideally a firearms examiner would be able to search the markings on bullets and cartridge cases against bullets and cartridge cases in a national database developed by police agencies throughout the country. In this way firearms transported across state lines and used to commit crimes could be tracked. This goal has been achieved to a large extent with the Combined DNA Indexing System (CODIS) in tracking sexual assault evidence (DNA) from state to state.

NIBIN begins by scanning the surface topography of a bullet or cartridge case. The instrument then makes a search against whatever database is available, and the computer produces a list of potential candidates for a match. The firearms examiner must then compare electronic images of the candidates against electronic images of the specimens under examination; in other words, the NIBIN computer does not make the comparison per se but provides a list of potential candidates for the examiner to look at and evaluate. Nevertheless, this results in substantial savings in effort and time. It is indeed an exciting moment when the firearms examiner makes a "cold hit," that is, locates a weapon already in the system that was responsible for firing the ammunition component of unknown origin found at the crime scene or recovered from the victim at autopsy. The event is so prized that it is even memorialized by the manufacturer of the NIBIN system with a plaque.

The firearms examiner must first become proficient at the examination and comparison of firearms and ammunition components. This allows the firearms examiner to answer properly the various questions that are associated with this type evidence, such as did this gun fire that bullet?

Once this level of expertise has been achieved, the firearms examiner may get additional training in shooting incident reconstruction to enhance further his or her skills. The combination of advanced training and significant field experience then adequately prepares an examiner for the rigors of courtroom presentation as to how a shooting likely occurred.

## LATENT PRINT EXAMINATION AND COMPARISON

The goal of fingerprint examination is to achieve individual identification, that is, to establish that a fingerprint came from a particular individual. The scientific basis for latent print identification consists of the following two premises:

1. The friction ridges formed during fetal development on the palmar surfaces of the hands and the plantar surfaces of the feet persist throughout the life of the individual except when damaged by scarring or disease.

2. No two areas of friction ridges on the hands or feet of any person or persons are duplicated.

The second premise is supported by the fingerprints of identical twins. Although DNA provides the instructions for producing every physical characteristic of the human body, the fingerprints of otherwise identical twins are different. Therefore, it must be concluded that fingerprint patterns are entirely random.

The examination of latent fingerprints involves several steps, progressing from simple to increasingly sophisticated. It begins with an initial visual inspection of the surface under strong light. Alternative light sources are then applied. Some prints will exhibit inherent luminescence when exposed to a laser or a forensic light source. Next the surface properties are evaluated for absorbency. One simply needs to imagine what a drop of water would do if placed on a given surface—remain intact or be absorbed. Fingerprint examiners generally process absorbent surfaces with chemical reagents and treat nonabsorbent with materials such as powder, superglue, or dyes.

Once the print has been enhanced through one mean or another, it must be photographed, lifted, or examined directly. As with firearms identification, fingerprint comparisons begin by determining whether class characteristics are consistent between samples. As previously discussed, there are three basic types of friction ridge detail: loops, whorls, and arches. These patterns constitute the class characteristics that the fingerprint examiner looks for. If, for example, the left thumb of the fingerprint from the crime scene is a loop pattern and the suspect is determined to have a whorl pattern for his or her left thumb, there is no need to look further at the suspect's prints. The suspect could not have left the latent print found at the crime scene.

A fingerprint card with the suspect's prints is the standard against which the questioned (crime scene) prints are compared. The comparison of class characteristics can be done without the aid of magnification when the prints being compared are clear and complete. When they are not clear or complete, the fingerprint examiner must then resort to a stereomicroscope or a hand lens, both of which have low-power magnification. The less detail that is visible, the more difficult this process will be.

Assuming that the class characteristics are consistent, the examiner then begins to look for the individual characteristics, or minutiae, discussed in chapter 2. There are six methods that can be used for the actual comparison: the overlay method, photographic strip method, Seymour trace method, polygon method, Osborn grid method, and conventional method.

The overlay method uses a transparent sheet printed with a fingerprint, usually with a different color ridge detail than the prints being compared with it. To determine identity or nonidentity, the fingerprint examiner lays the transparent sheet over the fingerprint sample. Obviously the base fingerprint and the overlay both must be to the same scale. The overlay transparency is then shifted back and forth and up and down as the examiner compares ridge detail.

The photographic strip method uses photographic enlargements of the two prints being compared. First the enlargement of the latent print is cut into lateral strips, then it is placed on top of the other enlargement and fixed in a secure frame. The strips are then removed and replaced one at a time to reveal the underlying detail on the inked impression. The visual comparison proceeds one strip at a time.

The Seymour trace method involves copying both the inked and the latent print onto tracing paper. The two tracings are then compared by overlaying them and using back lighting.

The polygon method utilizes photographic enlargements that are pinpoint punched at corresponding characteristics. The enlargements are then flipped over, and the analyst draws lines to connect the pinpoints. If the polygon created on both enlargements matches, an identification is declared.

The Osborn grid method involves making photographic enlargements of the two fingerprints to be compared with a superimposed grid on each. The grid cells are then compared cell by cell. If all available characteristics in each cell match, an identification is declared.

The conventional method has shown to be the best and most reliable method of comparison over the years. It involves a side-by-side visual comparison of the latent print and the fingerprint card using a fingerprint glass. The fingerprint glass consists of a magnifying lens mounted in a metal stand. This frees the examiner from having to hold the lens. The examiner begins by using a probe to mark a minutia observed in the print; the probe has a needle tip that is physically stuck into the print at the area of interest. A second fingerprint glass over the impression on the inked print card allows the examiner to look for the minutia observed in the questioned print. If the corresponding minutia is found, it is marked with a second probe. The examiner can then move back and forth between the questioned print and the inked impression from the suspect to confirm that the same detail is present. This process is repeated point by point until the examiner has obtained sufficient correspondence to make an identification.

With the advent of digital imaging the examiner can now do side-by-side comparisons on a monitor, as well as the overlays. Additionally, various software is available that allows questioned prints to be digitally enhanced. The software allows various points to be electronically marked and measurements of spatial orientation to be made on screen. The comparison results can then be printed and the print retained in the case file.

## THE LOW-TECH APPROACH TO FINGERPRINTS

Latent print residue that is deposited on the surface of nonabsorbent materials generally stays there and is not absorbed into the surface. This is adsorption, rather than absorption. The properties of the residue are different from the surface properties. This constitutes the basis for creating color differences through the selective absorption of powders and dyes.

Powders used for developing latent prints are of two general types: carbon and powdered iron. Fingerprint powder in the form of carbon black is the oldest and most widely used developing agent. The powder is applied using a brush that is twirled between the forefinger and thumb so that the bristle only very lightly contacts the surface with the print residue. The difference in surface characteristics usually is such that the print residue adsorbs the powder more readily than does the surrounding substrate. The result is that the print becomes more visible. The photograph shows a fingerprint brush, powder, and a developed print.

Carbon-based powders come in various textures in white, silver, gray, and black. Fluorescing powders of various colors are also available. The fluorescing powders are used with lasers and forensic light sources, which will be discussed in a following section.

Powdered iron filings are magnetic; they will stick to a magnet. By using a magnetic wand and powdered iron filings, a fingerprint "brush" can be created. When the magnetic wand is brushed across the surface, small amounts of the iron filings will adhere to the fingerprint residue. The advantage over the carbon powder method is easier cleanup (the magnetic wand can be used to pick up loose iron particles) and less interference by substrates. The powdered iron filings are marketed as magna powder. The wands have pull-up centers that demagnetize the wands to allow return of the magna powder to the container. The magna powder and wand are shown in the photograph.

Fingerprint brush, powder, and print (Courtesy of the author)

Magna powder and wand *(Courtesy of the author)*

Magna powder wands also come in large sizes so that large surface areas can be checked quickly. The large wands are useful for developing test impressions of footwear and tires using a special technique that involves first spraying the sole of the footwear or the tread of the tire with silicone.

Although the use of fingerprint powder or magna powder usually results in a greater degree of adsorbance by the fingerprint residue, there is often some adsorbance by the surface the fingerprint is on. This can be such a problem that the technique fails to provide sufficient contrast to be able to clearly distinguish the fingerprint. One simple way to overcome this is for the examiner to exhale very close to the fingerprint so as to have the moisture from the breath adhere to the fingerprint residue. This in turn results in more powder adhering to the residue. This may also be accomplished in a somewhat more sophisticated way by using a small steam iron to create the moisture.

In the early 1980s labs found that superglue (cyanoacrylate ester) adheres to fingerprint residue, particularly in a high-humidity environment. The superglue deposits on the friction ridges, turning them white. The examiner can then apply fingerprint powder or magna powder to

## Absence of Evidence Is Not Evidence of Absence

One of the most frequently contested subjects in court proceedings is the significance of not finding fingerprints on weapons, particularly firearms. Portrayals on television and in movies often suggest that fingerprints would have to be left on a gun or a knife if the person handled it. And defense attorneys, almost without exception, will use the absence of fingerprints on items to try to show that their client could not have committed the crime in question.

Yet, it is a mistake to attach any real significance to the absence of fingerprints. The statement "Absence of evidence is not evidence of absence," coined by bloodstain pattern analyst Herb McDonnell of Corning, New York, sums up this concept. "A positive statement cannot be made from a negative finding" is another way to say the same thing. Not finding a fingerprint means no more than just that: No fingerprints were found.

While juries are often persuaded to believe that fingerprints would have to be left on a gun or a knife if a person handled it, nothing could be further from the truth. Consider, for example, weapon design. The surfaces that are typically handled on weapons are by design textured so as not to be slippery. While it is certainly possible to leave a fingerprint on a weapon, in many instances it almost requires an overt effort to do so. Likewise, if a person had just washed and dried his or her hands prior to handling a weapon, it would be improbable that any fingerprints would be deposited. While it is still important always to test a weapon for fingerprints and not simply assume none will be found, it is more likely than not that the weapon will bear no fingerprints.

There are all sorts of explanations for why evidence might not be found, such as the following:

- It was never there to begin with.

- It was present but was removed prior to testing.

- The testing was improperly carried out.

The real point, again, is that negative evidence of any sort has no real significance beyond the fact that it was not found.

the print and get much greater adhesion of the powder. Another reason for using superglue development before powdering is that it allows the fingerprint examiner to view dark detail against a light background, which most people find easier. The fuming process takes place in a closed chamber, with the item that is to be superglue-fumed placed on a rack near the top of the chamber. The superglue is vaporized using a hot place inside the chamber, with a container of hot water also placed inside to increase the humidity. Large items, such as rifles, can be fumed inside superglue closets or large chambers specifically designed for this purpose. A typical small chamber is shown in the photograph.

Superglue fumes can be applied to the entire interior of a vehicle without requiring any special equipment if atmospheric conditions are appropriate. During hot summer months in areas with high humidity, all that is required is to put a small dish of superglue inside the closed vehicle and stand by for a while as Mother Nature does her thing. The entire interior surface of the vehicle will be coated with superglue fumes, developing latent prints in the process. The down side of this, of course, is that the vehicle interior and windows will then be covered with the residue, and it will be very difficult to remove. This method, therefore, is reserved for vehicles that are not likely to be returned to their owners and driven again.

Super glue chamber *(Courtesy of the author)*

Superglue wands that allow isolated fuming of objects are also available. These wands use butane (cigarette lighter fuel) to heat up and vaporize disks that are impregnated with superglue. The fumes so created emanate from the end of a tube, allowing the investigator to direct them onto the surface of interest. Superglue may thus be used at crime scenes without the need for a fume hood or other special equipment. This technique is also particularly useful when large, heavy objects, such as floor safes, need to be checked for latent prints.

## CHEMISTRY AND FINGERPRINTS

A variety of chemical reagents may be used to develop or enhance latent or partially visible prints. It is also possible to use various dyes or powders to make the prints visible to the unaided eye or to set the stage for producing fluorescence under certain wavelengths of light with lasers or forensic light sources. Because the chemical properties of latent fingerprints, if any, are unknown, the forensic fingerprint examiner must select the appropriate development method based on the substrate, the material on which a latent print may be deposited.

For instance, a number of reagents are specifically designed for use in developing prints on the adhesive side of tape. This is a very useful technology since criminals who immobilize victims often use tape, particularly duct tape. It is extremely difficult to get tape off a roll without touching the adhesive side, so the chances of finding the perpetrator's prints on the adhesive side of the tape are fairly good. Two common methods use gentian violet and sticky-side powder.

Gentian violet is a biological stain that is used to visualize latent prints on adhesive surfaces such as duct tape. The solution containing gentian violet is applied by spraying or dipping. It is a toxic substance and an irritant and as such must be handled with care and in a laboratory environment.

Sticky-side powder is a product specifically designed for use in developing latent prints on the adhesive side of tape. It is painted onto the adhesive side with a brush, allowed to remain there for 10 to 20 seconds, and then rinsed with water. A gray-black or white print will be developed. The product is nontoxic, and the surface can be reprocessed to further enhance the print. The development results from chemical adhesion of the powder particles to the fatty or oily deposits in the latent print.

Generally, however, the first step in latent print processing is to determine whether the substrate is porous or nonporous. The examiner can determine this merely by imagining what a drop of water would do if placed on the surface. If the surface would absorb water, the material is porous; if not, it is nonporous. For nonporous media powder (carbon black or iron filings), superglue, or a combination of powder and superglue will probably work best. For porous media the best chance for developing any latent prints that may be present involves sequential processing. It is also important to ascertain whether the prints were wet or dry when deposited. If the prints are the result of blood deposition, specialized development is required.

Treatments for substrates other than tape include small particle reagent and Sudan Black B. Small particle reagent is a suspension of molybdenum disulfide particles in water. This solution works as a kind of a liquid fingerprint powder by adhering to the fatty portion of the latent print residue. Small particle reagent works best on surfaces that are wet or have been wet. The particles form a gray coating on the fingerprint. The small particle reagent is applied by dipping or spraying. It is cheap, nontoxic, and easy to use.

Sudan Black B is a dye that stains the fatty components of latent prints to produce blue-black images. It can also be used to enhance superglue-developed images. Articles are treated by immersing them into the solution. After immersion the article is rinsed with water to remove excess dye. Sudan Black B is also cheap and nontoxic and can be used on contaminated surfaces.

The general processing of porous objects found at the crime scene involves a number of different methodologies. Whether the substrate being examined is paper, wood, leather, or some other porous material, a particular sequence must be followed for best results. This sequence begins with iodine fuming, followed by ninhydrin (alternatively, amido black or tetramethylbenzidine [TMB]), and then silver nitrate or physical developer.

Iodine crystals have the ability to go from the solid state directly into the gaseous state without ever becoming a liquid. This process

Print developed with iodine fumes *(Courtesy of the author)*

is known as sublimation. Iodine reacts with starch to produce a dark brown deposit. Fingerprint examiners started taking advantage of these two properties many years ago when they developed the technique of iodine fuming of porous materials such as paper. Iodine crystals are placed into a glass tube with plugs of glass wool on either end. A piece of rubber tubing is connected to one end to blow into. By holding the tube firmly in the hand during the process the examiner transfers sufficient heat to the iodine crystals to cause sublimation. When the iodine fumes contact the paper, they penetrate it deeply. If starch from a latent print is present, it reacts to produce a brown residue. This is not a permanent effect, so it must be photographed immediately. Iodine fuming is a useful technique for developing old fingerprints that have "soaked into" the paper over time. A fingerprint developed with iodine is shown in the photograph.

Ninhydrin is a protein dye that may be applied after iodine fuming has been attempted. Latent prints frequently contain amino acids. Ninhydrin reacts with amino acids and proteins to produce a deep violet color. (If one happens to get some of the ninhydrin solution on their

Print developed with ninhydrin *(Courtesy of the author)*

hands, they will have purple stains for several days.) The ninhydrin is usually applied as a solution in alcohol or petroleum ether. It is sprayed on, or the item of interest is immersed in the solution. The use of steam or heat speeds up the development process, which can sometimes take overnight. The prints must be photographed to preserve the results. Ninhydrin will also enhance prints in blood since protein will be present. Ninhydrin must be handled with care although it is not highly toxic. A print developed with ninhydrin is shown in the photograph.

Two other chemical reagents that are also effective in the enhancement of bloody prints are amido black and TMB. Like ninhydrin, amido black is a protein stain. TMB, on the other hand, reacts with the hemoglobin molecule in the blood to produce a colored product.

Silver nitrate reacts with salt to produce a dark colored residue. Since salt is often part of the latent print residue, this reaction allows yet another way of development or enhancement of prints. It must follow ninhydrin if sequential enhancements will be applied. If salt is present in the substrate, the entire object will darken. Silver nitrate reacts with light to darken also. In fact, silver nitrate is the principal reactive material in

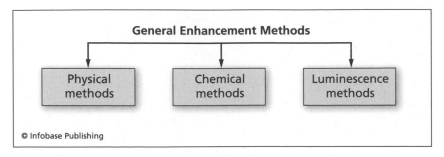

General approach for enhancing latent fingerprints

black-and-white film, in which the brightest areas show up darkest on the film (hence the term *negative*).

The last reagent in the sequence is physical developer. Physical developer often replaces silver nitrate in the sequential processing scheme since it is silver nitrate based and thus reacts with salts. Use of physical developer is the only technique to show adequate results on paper items that have gotten wet. It also can be used to detect footwear impressions on paper items. Some of the various approaches to developing latent prints are illustrated in the accompanying flow charts.

The use of chemical properties to develop latent prints has its limits. Developing fingerprints on bodies, for example, is a topic that always generates tremendous interest. Strangulation and other crimes involving physical contact between the victim and the perpetrator raise the question of whether identifiable fingerprints can be located on human tissue. Different methods, such as dusting with powder and using iodine fuming, have been tried over the years. Although success rates remain very low, the current method of choice is superglue fuming followed by dusting with magnetic powder that has been stained with Rhodamine. A laser or other light source is then used to visualize the print. Hairless areas of the body are more likely to yield identifiable prints.

Rhodamine is a stain that is used primarily to enhance the luminescence of latent prints that have been treated with the cyanoacrylate (superglue-fuming) procedure. Rhodamine 6G is very useful for this purpose because it produces fluorescence in the presence of lasers and forensic light sources. This fluorescence aids in the visualization, especially when background interference is a problem. A spray or rinse bottle is filled with methyl alcohol or distilled water and a

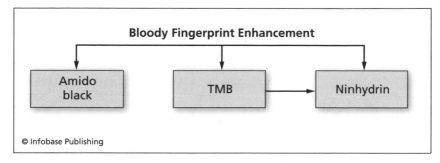

Enhancing bloody fingerprints

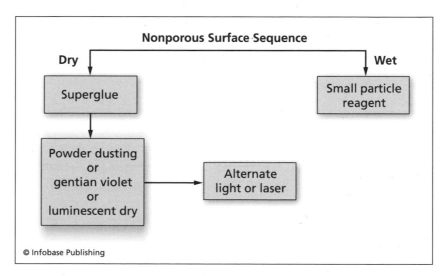

Developing fingerprints on nonporous substrates

small amount of Rhodamine 6G added. The Rhodamine solution is then applied to the surface of interest. When light of the appropriate wavelength (450–525 nanometers) is introduced, areas that have absorbed the dye will fluoresce. Typically fingerprint residue that has been "coated" with superglue will absorb more dye than the surrounding substrate and result in enhanced visualization. Rhodamine 6G is thought to be relatively safe in small amounts. It must never be ingested or inhaled, however.

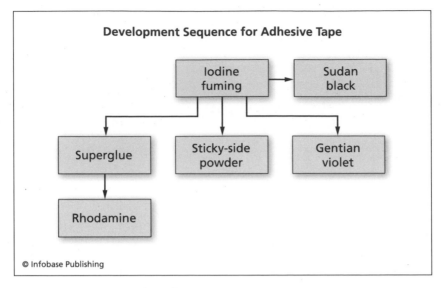

Developing fingerprints on adhesive tape

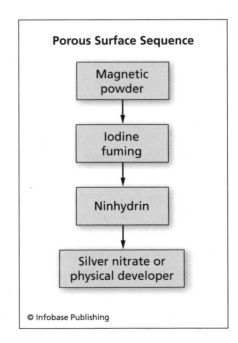

Developing latent fingerprints on porous surfaces

The fingerprint examiner has no way of knowing which of a variety of possible fingerprint residue components may be present and in what amount. The availability of numerous fingerprint development techniques increases the chance that the examiner will isolate the latent prints.

## FINGERPRINTS AND MODERN TECHNOLOGY

Advances in technology have gradually contributed to fingerprint examiners' efficiency in developing, enhancing, recording, and comparing fingerprints. Using fluorescence to develop latent prints, examiners can find more prints, more easily. As discussed in the previous section, lasers and forensic light sources can both produce inherent fluorescence and stimulate it in fluorescing powders and dyes. Taken together, these techniques represent one of the most significant developments in the field ever.

Similarly, reflected ultraviolet light can be used to enhance latent prints. The National Police Agency of Japan pioneered this method, and a commercially available system is marketed under the acronym RUVIS. Several laboratories, including the NYPD lab, have purchased this equipment and begun to evaluate it.

Magnification is useful as a fingerprint enhancement, and technology has made extremely high magnification possible. Typically, however, excessive magnification creates more problems than it solves when it comes to viewing fingerprints. Since the scanning electron microscope is capable of incredibly high magnification, on the order of 400,000X or more, it would not appear to be a likely candidate for use in visualizing or enhancing latent prints. However, by using low magnifications of latent prints developed using small particle reagents, some very good results have been obtained.

Electronic fingerprint enhancement is one area that modern digital imaging and high-speed computers have facilitated. Economical and readily available software such as Adobe Photoshop allow the electronic enhancement of vague fingerprints or the removal of interfering background patterns. Many times simply adjusting brightness and contrast of scanned images of fingerprints can provide adequate enhancement to be able to identify the source of a fingerprint.

A type of technology that eliminates a step in the fingerprint recording process is the Livescan fingerprint. This is a fingerprint obtained electronically without the intermediate step of getting an impression on paper. A number of different technologies have been adapted to accomplish this, all of which rely on the sensing of differences in the ridges and valleys that make up the friction ridge detail. These technologies include thermal sensing, ultrasonic reflection, optical reflection, and differential capacitance. The most popular Livescan technology relies on optical reflectance. The equipment is quite simple to use, requiring only that the finger be placed on a glass scanner that is part of the case housing the hardware; however, this technology is still in its early stages and has yet to replace inked fingerprints.

There is a tedium associated with the visual comparison of fingerprints that surpasses other areas of physical evidence due to the quantity of prints each examiner must deal with on a daily basis. Ever since law-enforcement agencies began using fingerprints to identify criminals, there has been a need to streamline this tedious task. Despite many ingenious methods that have been developed to increase the efficiency of the manual indexing and searching of fingerprints, visual comparison has remained very time consuming.

The development of digital imaging and the high-speed computer set the stage for law-enforcement agencies to explore ways to automate some or all of the comparison details involved with fingerprint evidence. The comparison of fingerprints involves two steps: First the fingerprint of interest must be compared against literally millions of others, and second, if a candidate is found, verification is required. Clearly, using a computer would have the greatest impact on workload in the first step, where multiple comparisons are required. An automated fingerprint identification system, AFIS, which compares electronically generated fingerprint data, was the result of this need.

## THE FINGERPRINT EXAMINER AT THE CRIME SCENE

Without a doubt the fingerprint examiner has more than enough to do within the laboratory without having to seek more responsibilities outside the laboratory. Nonetheless, it is extremely desirable for the fingerprint examiner to be at the crime scene. This is because the fingerprint examiner is the only person capable of assessing a fingerprint's potential identification value. If present, the examiner can decide at the scene whether a fingerprint is worthy of enhancement or if on-scene enhancement is sufficient.

It is certainly true that crime scene personnel who are not qualified as fingerprint comparison experts can locate, develop, and document (photograph and/or lift) fingerprints. The best-case scenario, however, is that the fingerprint examiner accomplishes the entire process from start to finish. For one thing this means that only one person has to give court testimony about fingerprint evidence. For another having one less person in the chain of custody of the evidence minimizes the possibility of its loss or contamination.

There are times when having the fingerprint examiner at the scene is critical. One example is when crucial fingerprint evidence must be collected at the scene because the object the print is on is not readily removable. Another instance is when investigators need to eliminate prints belonging to persons with legitimate access to the scene in order to isolate prints that possibly belong to suspects. Ultimately the fingerprint examiner is the person who will be making the comparison of any fingerprints recovered to any suspects. The location and documentation of fingerprints at the crime scene can therefore become an issue at trial, and the fingerprint examiner is the most logical person to testify about such issues.

Because of the necessity to document fingerprint evidence photographically, it is not uncommon for fingerprint examiners to have expertise in photography. This makes for a good situation at crime scenes, since one person can do both the photography and the fingerprint work. Because fingerprint examiners are trained to pay attention to minute details, they make excellent crime scene investigators in general.

## THE AUTOMATED FINGERPRINT IDENTIFICATION SYSTEM

In the early days of fingerprinting law-enforcement agencies began "booking" fingerprints taken from individuals arrested for crimes so that the records would be readily available. They also began to maintain leftover latent prints so that they might be compared with existing and future additions to the fingerprint files.

The first law-enforcement agencies to develop fingerprint collections were large ones, such as the NYPD, LAPD, and FBI. These agencies sponsored rigorous research into how best to carry out scientific comparison of fingerprints. They subsequently developed strong training programs for maximum efficiency. Nevertheless, the sheer numbers of fingerprints flowing into these departments soon overwhelmed them. These agencies had rooms full of filing cabinets crammed with fingerprint cards. Without the Henry system of classification the task of cataloging and organizing the fingerprints into any kind of usable file would have been hopeless.

The traditional method for processing a new fingerprint card was to classify each of the 10 fingerprints of the individual, then search the files for a duplicate card, if any. Once it was determined that the prints were "new," the next step was to compare them to the file of latent prints from unsolved cases. A fingerprint examiner might spend hours with these tasks. The process was even more laborious if a single latent print, without the remaining fingerprints of the hand to help narrow the field, was brought in for identification, because many more comparisons would be needed.

The pressure of case demands combined with the tedious and time-consuming process of manual comparison made for a very undesirable work environment. All this prompted agencies to look for some relief in the form of automation through electronic media and digital imaging. The tremendous success of fingerprint identification technology has ushered in a whole new era in law enforcement, to say nothing of turning a boring job into a high-tech profession.

An AFIS works like this: A latent fingerprint that cannot be defined as to which hand (left versus right) or finger comes into the fingerprint unit. The fingerprint examiner scans and enters the fingerprint into the system. The software then compares the fingerprint with all the fingerprints in the system. If the software finds one or more possible matches, it reports them in descending order of probability, that is, the most likely candidate is reported first and the less like candidates follow in the listing. The first diagram shows the flow of a fingerprint through the fingerprint identification process, including AFIS.

This automation cuts out a huge amount of labor for the fingerprint examiner, but it does not eliminate his or her job. The actual identification at the end of the process must be carried out by the examiner, not by the machine. The machine is not capable of making the final judgment, which must be based on experience and training as well as visual appearances. At the beginning of the process, too, only human expertise will do. Before it can be put into the system, the latent print must first be evaluated as to whether it is "AFIS quality," which requires visual evaluation by the examiner. If enhancement is appropriate, the examiner must perform this as well.

As shown in the second diagram, the AFIS consists of three steps or stages: data sensing (of the fingerprint), data extraction (of the sensed

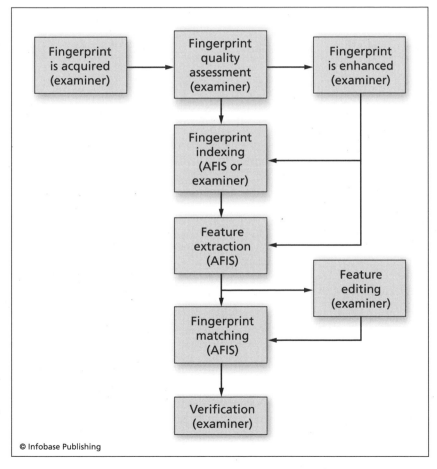

© Infobase Publishing

The flow of a fingerprint through the fingerprint unit

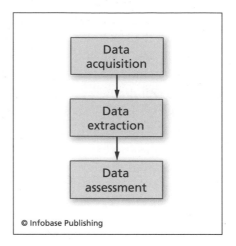

Automated fingerprint
identification system (AFIS)
flow chart

© Infobase Publishing

data), and comparison evaluation (the machine evaluates the quality of the "match"). The AFIS may be set to accept or reject a certain threshold of comparison quality. In this way the examiner can increase or reduce the number of possible matches the machine offers.

It is important for the reader to understand that AFIS is a process and not a particular brand name of equipment. There are a number of manufacturers of AFIS equipment, and different manufacturers rely on different systems for comparison. For example, one system may base identification on multiple impressions of the same finger, while another uses multiple different fingers of the same hand. The quality of the AFIS systems currently on the market has improved dramatically over the years. At its inception AFIS were stand-alone systems that could not communicate with one another. If two neighboring agencies purchased AFIS equipment from different manufacturers, each was unable to search the other's database (a problem analogous to the PC-Macintosh situation). This has changed somewhat, making communication between different systems more feasible.

A continuing problem is data storage. Too much data in AFIS, like too much data in a personal computer's hard drive, causes the system to become sluggish. As with written data, compression of fingerprint images is the first solution. There has been some success with this, but research is currently being done to improve matters.

Most of the problems associated with AFIS comparisons, however, can be attributed to the data acquisition step. This is the old "garbage in equals garbage out" problem. Recall that the friction ridge detail of a person's hands is three-dimensional: It has length, width, and depth. Fingerprinting, however, does not record depth, and scanning methods affect the consistency of the two-dimensional image that is recorded. One method of entering fingerprints into the database is through live scanning, where the fingers are pressed directly onto a glass plate. Slight differences in pressure of the finger can cause apparent changes in the appearance in two dimensions. Likewise, nonuniform contact can cause distortion. Cuts, burns, and other damage, either temporary or

## To Err Is Human

All humans make mistakes; however, there is zero tolerance for mistakes in forensic science. How then can humans be involved? The resolution to this apparent paradox is a system of checks, balances, and strict guidelines. With fingerprint identification a key requirement is that all identifications must be verified by another examiner. But does that always work? The answer is most of the time, but not always, as the following story illustrates.

On March 11, 2004, terrorist bombings in Madrid, Spain, killed 191 people and injured 2,000. An investigation produced a plastic bag containing the detonator, and latent fingerprints were recovered from the plastic bag. The Spanish National Police provided the FBI with photographic images of the latent fingerprints, and the FBI lab in Quantico, Virginia, used AFIS to search 4–5 million print records for possible matches to the fingerprints. One of the fingerprints was linked by AFIS to a Portland, Oregon, lawyer named Brandon Mayfield, as reported in the *Oregonian* newspaper.

According to the regional news Web site OregonLive.com, the FBI had asked Spanish authorities for the original evidence when the digital images first arrived in March 2004 but got no response. The FBI proceeded with the comparison, and ultimately an FBI examiner determined that the print belonged to Mayfield. At least three additional

*(continues)*

permanent, can result in other problems for the AFIS machine as it tries to compare fingerprints. In addition, electronic sensing adds "noise" that can distort fingerprint images. Anyone who has scanned images and then tried to print them or project them through a multimedia projector has experienced this phenomenon to one degree or another.

Interestingly the AFIS was developed to use the same processes that the fingerprint examiner uses in manually comparing fingerprints, but

*(continued)*

FBI examiners subsequently verified the identification. The court also appointed an independent examiner, not employed by the FBI, to examine the fingerprint, and he agreed that the fingerprint belonged to Mayfield. It should be pointed out that the database includes not only criminals but also anyone who has ever served in the military or worked in law enforcement or a security position. In this case public records show that Mayfield was arrested for burglary in Wichita, Kansas, on December 22, 1984, in addition to having served in the army.

Prior to the AFIS "hit," law-enforcement officers had no reason to believe Mayfield had any involvement in the bombings. The investigation commenced solely on the basis of the fingerprint. By mid-April 2004 Spanish officials were questioning whether the print was Mayfield's. In response the FBI sent a team of fingerprint examiners to Madrid to view the evidence directly only to learn it had been destroyed.

According to a motion filed in the U.S. district court in Oregon, Spanish officials ultimately linked the latent print to a different individual and the FBI began a reexamination. Two FBI latent print examiners flew to Spain to examine the best possible digital image maintained by Spanish officials. Four additional FBI examiners back in Quantico, Virginia, then joined the effort. On May 24, 2004, the FBI withdrew its previous fingerprint identification.

the machine cannot compensate for complex visual textures, sweat pores, or ridge thickness, all of which can be factored in by the human examiner. Without the benefit of the "art" the human examiner has developed over years of training and experience, AFIS evaluation is incomplete.

The public tends to put more faith in computers than in people because, as everyone knows, humans make mistakes. There is a notion that AFIS is foolproof, but it is not. After all, humans made computers, and a human must make the ultimate decision as to fingerprint identification or nonidentification. So, errors can and sometimes do happen. High-profile cases, by their very nature, draw lots of interest and publicity, and when an error has been made on a fingerprint case, it tends to distort the perceived accuracy of the field. In fact, the error rate for fingerprint identification, whether assisted by AFIS or not, has been very low through the years.

The goal of forensic evidence is the identification of the perpetrator of a crime. Firearms and fingerprint evidence both offer the opportunity for positive identification. Firearms identification is limited to identifying the responsible firearm or ammunition component, while fingerprint identification is capable of identifying the responsible individual. The combination of firearms and fingerprint evidence offers insight into both who committed a crime and how that crime may have been committed.

# 4

# Forensic Applications

In the context of firearms and fingerprint examinations forensic applications exclusively involve crime scene reconstructions. The goal of the reconstruction of a shooting incident is to establish a probable or likely sequence of events related to the shooting, while recognizing that other explanations are possible. Crime scene reconstruction is valuable not only for analyzing what could have happened during the incident but also for identifying what could not have happened.

## RECONSTRUCTING SHOOTINGS USING FIREARMS-RELATED EVIDENCE AT THE SCENE

The reconstruction of a shooting incident is the ultimate challenge for the criminal investigator. This is arguably the most important aspect of the scene investigation. In most large police departments this will be a combined effort involving the firearms examiner, the crime scene investigator, and the lead detective. Typically the firearms examiner possesses expertise regarding firearms and ammunition components that neither the detective nor the crime scene investigator possesses. Likewise, the detective and the crime scene investigator both possess special skills of their own. The combination of these skills results in a powerful force for uncovering what took place at a crime scene and how to document and present it.

In smaller departments manpower constraints may mean that one person does the bulk of the reconstruction work. While this is a formidable task, it is certainly not beyond the abilities of many capable individuals working in smaller agencies throughout the country. Obviously more time is involved from start to finish when fewer people are involved in the effort.

The author has been conducting training classes in shooting incident reconstruction to police agencies for 30 years. These classes typically enroll a combination of firearms examiners, crime scene investigators, and detectives. This is an ideal class makeup since it allows all of the potential participants in a reconstruction to discuss areas of mutual concern and to learn more about one another's roles.

On the job the firearms examiner will be able to recognize when things do not seem to fit in a shooting scene. Being able to recognize early in the investigative process, for example, that the presence of characteristic fluted chamber marks suggests that a cartridge case was fired in a fully automatic weapon can be important thanks to having the familiarity and understanding of firearms and ammunition components that others at the scene probably do not have.

The reconstruction of a shooting incident requires both on-scene examinations and evaluations as well as laboratory testing. Laboratory testing involves the use of specialized equipment, such as microscopes, and chemical testing, such as gunshot residue testing, that cannot practically be carried out at the crime scene. Health hazards associated with most types of chemical testing further dictate that this testing be done in a laboratory environment.

## THE CRIME LAB'S ROLE IN SHOOTING RECONSTRUCTION

Not all of the reconstruction of a shooting incident is done at the scene. A substantial part is often done off scene at the crime laboratory. For example, trace evidence and gunshot residue are documented in the lab; firearms testing is also laboratory work.

It is not uncommon for fired bullets recovered at crime scenes and from shooting victims to have tiny bits of material adhering to their surfaces as a result of striking things. This material is generally described as trace evidence. Typical trace evidence recovered from fired bullets includes blood, hair, tissue, fibers, paint, wood, glass, and so forth. With hollow-point bullets, which have a cavity in the nose, it is particularly common for this type of evidence to be present. As such a bullet goes through various different layers before it finally stops, tiny fragments are built up within the cavity. The result is a veritable "archaeological history" of where the bullet has been. Soft lead bullets are also prone to collect material on their surfaces. Even though the firearms examiner may not have the expertise to analyze and identify this trace evidence, recognizing its importance and getting the proper person involved are important parts of the job.

Gunshot residue testing is conducted to determine the approximate distance of a shot. This testing requires the use of chemicals and other items that are part of a laboratory environment.

As described in chapter 3, when a firearm is discharged, a cone of debris exits the end of the barrel behind the bullet or shot pellets. This debris consists of soot and gunpowder particles. The soot, being lighter, travels only a foot or so at most. The gunpowder particles travel varying distances depending on their shape. Spherical or ball powder travels the farthest and disk or flake powder the least distance. Flattened ball powder falls in between. In general, gunpowder particles are expected to strike anything within arm's length of the end of the barrel.

The amount of soot produced as well as the amount and distribution of gunpowder particles vary by manufacturer and by load. For example, two different brands of cartridges of the same design fired from the same distance may produce different residue patterns, as shown in the photograph.

A blissfully ignorant person might assume that one shot was fired from a different distance than the other, when in fact they were both fired from the same distance using different brands of ammunition. Once again, this is why it is important to have a well-trained examiner involved in the examination and interpretation of the evidence.

Precision target shooters are aware that consistent results depend on consistent loads and are careful to ensure that everything they can

## Ignorance Is Not Bliss

The old saying that "Ignorance is bliss" may be true in some instances, but it is certainly not so in a shooting incident. Ignorance of various aspects of physical evidence and their ramifications can lead to false assumptions and distort the truth.

Consider the following case, which the author reviewed in the early 1990s. A man was charged with intentionally shooting a 12-year-old girl in the head, killing her, during an altercation with a group of individuals at a housing project. The defendant admitted having fired several shots into the ground in an effort to keep the group at bay but was adamant that he had not fired intentionally at the girl.

The location of fired cartridge cases found at the scene seemed to contradict where the defendant claimed he was standing. This was based on the fact that most semiautomatic weapons eject fired cartridge cases rearward and to the right. The defendant was firing a Chinese SKS 7.62 × 39 semiautomatic rifle loaded with Chinese-manufactured ammunition, consisting of bullets with an inner steel post surrounded by a lead core and a steel outer jacket.

Other physical evidence, however, was consistent with the defendant's claim. There were some apparent bullet strike marks on the ground in front of where the young girl had fallen. In fact, a bullet was discovered in the ground at one of the marks. It was flattened on one side. Another bullet was recovered from the girl's head, and it too was flattened on one side. The bullet had entered the girl's forehead resulting in a large, irregular wound. Given the construction of the bullet (which in effect constituted armor-piercing ammunition) and the fact that the 7.62 × 39 rifle is a high-velocity weapon, it seemed very strange that the bullet did not pass completely through the girl's head. To someone with firearms knowledge this would suggest that the bullet had much less energy than what would be expected.

An additional "red flag" was the irregular shape of the entry wound in the girl's forehead. Bullets produce holes that are either round or oval

*(continues)*

*(continued)*

shaped, depending on whether the bullet strikes at a 90-degree angle or something significantly less, and trained firearms examiners are familiar with this fact. Irregular bullet holes and wounds are indicative of a bullet that has been destabilized as a result of striking something else first.

When a bullet strikes something and either passes through it or ricochets, it loses a great deal of its energy (something on the order of 40 percent is not uncommon). In this case the fact that the bullet failed to exit the girl's skull combined with the irregular entrance wound suggested that an intermediary target was involved. The flattened bullet recovered at autopsy, along with the bullet strike marks observed on the ground between the girl's location and the defendant's, provided still more evidence of something other than a straight-on shot.

By reconstructing the shooting using a tripod-mounted laser the examiner determined that the angle of ricochet required to strike the girl was of the order of six degrees. That angle is within the range that would be expected for a ricochet off hard ground. A little knowledge also cleared up the apparent conflict between the location of the fired cartridge cases and the reported position of the shooter: An SKS rifle ejects fired cartridge cases forward rather than back and to the right rear like most firearms. In other words, there was no real conflict.

This case is a good example of the importance of having a knowledgeable firearms examiner present at a crime scene. Without proper training and knowledge it is easy to be blissfully ignorant. But incorrect interpretation of a crime scene can have very serious consequences, as people's lives often hinge on the results of investigations. In this particular case the defendant ended up being charged with negligent homicide rather than first-degree murder.

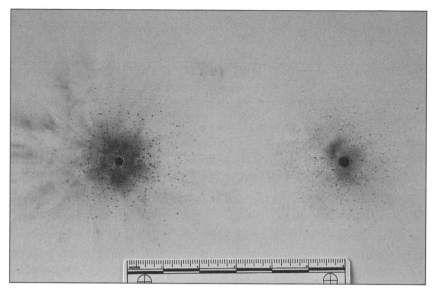

Soot and gunpowder deposits from different brands of ammunition
*(Courtesy of the author)*

control is the same. Criminals, on the other hand, are seldom picky about ammunition and frequently use more than one brand in the same weapon. Usually their only concern is to carry out the crime they are involved in. Besides, most shootings take place within a few feet, where small differences in load are unlikely to affect the deadliness of a shot.

Another area of shooting reconstruction for which the crime laboratory environment is required is the testing of firearms for proper functioning. An issue that frequently comes up is the possible accidental discharge of a weapon in a shooting incident. Investigators often hear the phrase "the gun went off." The only way to substantiate or refute the statement is through laboratory examination and testing.

There are three ways that firearms can be discharged: intentionally, unintentionally, and accidentally. Intentional discharge is self-explanatory: Someone pulls the trigger on purpose. Unintentional discharge results from something other than a mechanical malfunction. Accidental discharge results from a mechanical malfunction.

The difference between unintentional discharge and accidental discharge can be nebulous. Things like a sympathetic nervous response or a reaction to surprise can result in the unintentional discharge of firearms, but these matters are beyond the scope of a crime laboratory examination.

Mechanical function or malfunction, however, is ascertained through laboratory examination and testing of firearms. The following are the typical questions associated with this type of testing:

- Will the gun fire upon being dropped?

- Will the gun fire upon the bolt closing?

- Will the gun fire fully automatic?

- Will the gun fire as a result of the slide (part of the action on a semi-automatic) being released without pulling the trigger?

- Will the gun fire as a result of the hammer being pulled back partially and then released?

- Does the gun have a "hair trigger"?

The term *hair trigger* refers to an excessively light trigger pull. Trigger pull is the amount of force required on the trigger in order to fire a weapon. Depending on weapon types and designs, trigger pulls between four and 14 pounds are considered normal. Trigger pulls between two and four pounds are considered light. Trigger pulls below two pounds, and particularly below one pound, are referred to as "hair triggers."

The lighter the trigger pull, the more prone a weapon is to unintentional firing. This is why police agencies typically require their service weapons to have at least eight-pound trigger pulls. The NYPD takes this a step further by requiring their weapons have 12-pound trigger pulls.

It is not uncommon for individuals who are unfamiliar with firearms to claim "the gun just went off by itself." Firearms examiners and others with some knowledge of firearms recognize the impossibility of such an event, but it is true that broken or worn internal parts can make firearms unreliable and dangerous. A "backyard gunsmith" who attempts to improve the gun's action or to convert semiautomatic weapons to fire fully automatic can cause the same result. The determination of these conditions requires disassembly in the laboratory by a trained firearms examiner.

## THE CRIME LAB'S ROLE IN CRIMINAL INVESTIGATION

In criminal investigation the first duty of the investigator is to determine whether or not a crime has been committed. This involves evaluating whether a suspect's testimony is consistent with the lab results. Results of

### Ironclad Alibi

A young man with no prior criminal record was arrested for shooting his girlfriend in the head. According to the defendant, he kept a revolver in a nightstand beside the bed. He and his girlfriend had been arguing in the bedroom, he said, and she had made a move toward the drawer where the gun was but he beat her to it. They then faced each other as he held the gun down at his right side. At this point, he stated, she grabbed an iron from the ironing board with her right hand and swung it from left to right at his head. He ducked and raised his hand that was holding the gun to ward off the blow, he said. Instinctively he clenched his hand when the iron struck the barrel of the gun. At that point the gun fired and shot the victim in the head.

When the weapon was examined by the firearms examiner, it was determined to have a trigger pull of only 1.5 pounds. According to the defendant he had cut the trigger spring to lighten the trigger pull for target shooting, a fairly common practice. An examination of the iron revealed what appeared to be soot on the side. Also present were tiny droplets of blood consistent with a gunshot. All of this was consistent with the defendant's version of events; nonetheless, the jury found the defendant guilty.

Whether firing is unintentional or intentional, as the jury in this case apparently believed, a hair trigger greatly increases the chance that a shot will be fired.

lab testing can either support a defendant's explanation or rule it out. Lab results that are consistent with an individual's explanation of suspicious circumstances support the idea that he or she was telling the truth.

Whether the defendants involved were actually telling the truth about what happened or just make a lucky guess is a different matter. Over the years the author has investigated several cases involving discharge of firearms in which lab results cleared defendants who were initially charged with a criminal offense. In one of these cases a biker was charged with shooting his female companion. According to the biker, they had pulled over and were taking a little break from their ride off the road in a rural area. The biker stated that he had a 380 semiautomatic pistol with him, and he had taken it out to shoot at a can. His companion, he said, was seated across from him on a rock. As he cocked the gun, he claimed it slipped out of his hand and fell to the ground, striking a rock and discharging the bullet that struck his companion.

When the pistol was brought into the crime laboratory, examiners tested it to determine whether it would discharge if dropped. Given the way the shooting allegedly took place, the gun would have had to have landed butt first against the rock. Testing revealed that the gun would accidentally fire when dropped butt first while cocked. Charges against the biker were then dropped, there being no other evidence against him.

In another case a man claimed that he and a second man were struggling over a sawed-off shotgun. The defendant said he was holding the shotgun with his right hand on the stock and his left hand around the back of the barrel, in front of the hammer, when the other man jerked forward. According to the defendant, this caused his left hand to slide back across the hammer, releasing the hammer and causing the gun to discharge, killing the second man.

Testing on the weapon confirmed that it would fire if the hammer was pulled back partially and released. Once again, the defendant was released because there was no further evidence to indicate that the shooting was not an accident, just as he had claimed.

Sometimes firearms examination assists in a criminal investigation even though no shots were fired. In one such case a man was arrested following an altercation with a police officer. The officer stated that the man had pointed the weapon at him and "may have pulled the trigger," although the gun did not fire. A check of the weapon by the investigating officer revealed a live round under the hammer with what appeared to be a light or partial firing pin impression. This finding seemed to support the idea that the hammer had been released (that is, the trigger had been pulled) and had struck the cartridge but failed to fire the bullet (that is, had misfired). Closer examination of the weapon by the firearms examiner, however, revealed that the firing pin protruded above the breech face plane slightly. This was just enough to produce a light firing pin impression on the primer of a round in the chamber but not enough to produce firing. Thus the firearms examiner was able to show that the light firing pin impression present on the cartridge case was not necessarily indicative of a misfire. By also firing several test rounds the firearms examiner was able to show the impact of the firing pin produced a significantly different mark. This was critical in showing the man was innocent.

In a similar case investigated by the author a man had reportedly pointed a revolver at two people and pulled the trigger, but the gun had not fired in either case. Police later arrested a suspect who had a revolver in his possession. There were two cartridges in the weapon with light marks on their primers. When tested in the crime lab, the weapon would occasionally misfire (fail to fire). This finding substantiated the allegations against the suspect.

Another longtime category of crime lab work is fingerprint examination. Historically, the question of whether a person handled a firearm required the presence of fingerprints that were identifiable to the person in question. But advances in DNA technology have overcome the need for identifiable fingerprints in many cases. When there is physical contact between an object and a person, there is a good chance that skin cells (epithelial cells) will be deposited. Since all nucleated cells, such as epithelial cells, have DNA present, it is possible to isolate and identify that DNA to the contributor. Thus, if a person merely handles a firearm, it is possible to show that person has been in contact with the firearm.

Ammunition and other objects involved in crimes are equally appropriate for determining whether DNA is present. For example, the crime lab can ascertain whether there is evidence that a person handled cartridges loaded into a weapon. Evidence like this can help prove or disprove a crime.

Finally, the trace evidence section of the crime lab often has the opportunity to play a vital role in criminal investigation. In a somewhat

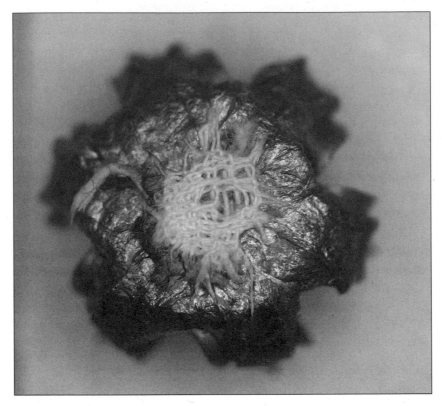

Fibers embedded in a bullet *(Courtesy of the author)*

unusual trace evidence case the author was involved in, a shot was fired at a robbery suspect, and the bullet was recovered. The bullet had passed through the suspect's jacket and wound up on the floor. The robber fled the scene. Upon examination of the bullet the crime lab observed that some coarse white fibers were embedded in the nose of the bullet. When a suspect was arrested several days later, police recovered a white jacket from his vehicle. A comparison of the jacket fabric to the fibers on the bullet showed them to be similar microscopically and chemically. The suspect was convicted largely on the basis of the fiber evidence.

Physical evidence has taken on an enhanced role in legal proceedings as a result of the increased public awareness of this evidence and their associated expectations as a result of the saturation of the airways with "CSI-related" drama. Juries not only expect to be presented with physical evidence but in some cases have failed to convict based on a perceived shortcoming on the part of the state in not pursuing some trivial bit of "evidence." The trial of actor Robert Blake in California in 2005 is a classic example of this "CSI effect." Jurors stated that they acquitted Blake due to the lab not having found gunshot residue on his hands. Clearly the state did a poor job in educating the jury regarding "Absence of evidence is not evidence of absence." Accordingly, crime laboratories must rigorously examine all evidence having any potential probative value as well as carefully explain the significance, or lack thereof, of not finding certain evidence.

## THE ROLE OF FINGERPRINTS IN CRIME SCENE RECONSTRUCTION

Fingerprints are the oldest and most recognized form of personal identification used in law enforcement. More crimes have been solved through fingerprint identification than by any other means. As previously discussed, however, identifiable fingerprints seldom show up on firearms or ammunition. This can be problematic because juries expect fingerprints to be present whenever firearms are involved in crimes. Television and movies have perpetuated the myth that fingerprints will be found on every surface. For instance, in one episode of a television show that featured a seemingly inept detective who always solved cases in a brilliant fashion, the murderer had worn latex gloves to avoid leaving fingerprints at the scene. The detective solved the case by cutting the gloves open and dusting the inside surfaces with ground-up pencil lead, revealing the killer's fingerprints inside the gloves.

Although the real world differs significantly from Hollywood, fingerprints still provide a very important means for reconstructing crimes. First and foremost, fingerprints put an individual at the crime scene. Nevertheless, it must be remembered that not finding fingerprints cannot be interpreted to mean an individual was not at the scene.

Second, fingerprints can put an individual in a particular position or location at the scene. This can be the difference between being found guilty or innocent of a particular crime. Suppose, for example, a person has been accused of striking and killing another person with a bat based on the presence of fingerprints on the bat. The suspect offers the explanation that he had touched and moved the bat after finding it lying across the chest of the dead man but steadfastly maintains that he was not the killer. If the fingerprints are in a position to support touching but not holding, then that would be a huge part of his defense. On the other hand, if the fingerprints are more consistent with holding the bat than merely touching it, the defendant would have a big problem.

Fingerprints can put a person behind the steering wheel of a vehicle, put a knife in someone's hand, prove that they were on the floor at some point, suggest that they opened a drawer, and on and on. As long as the identification is valid and the individual has no legitimate reason to have been at the scene, the evidence is irrefutable.

Criminal investigators frequently use fingerprint evidence as a ploy to gain confessions from people they are interrogating. This tactic has been used successfully many times. The suspect is brought into the interrogation room and confronted with a question, such as "How did your fingerprints get on the murder weapon?" Suspects who have something to hide frequently fall for the ruse and start talking. The Supreme Court has ruled that police agencies may legitimately use deception to gain confessions.

The general knowledge that fingerprints are so incriminating often results in criminals making statements to investigators as to why their fingerprints will be present. In a highly publicized murder case in the Dallas, Texas, area, a woman had called 911 to report that her two young sons had been stabbed by an intruder. As she spoke to the 911 operator, seemingly hysterical, she mentioned that she had touched the murder weapon and that her fingerprints "would probably be there," a strange thing to be concerned about as her two sons lay dying. The jury may have perceived her remark as an attempt to cover up her crime. In any event she was convicted.

The general knowledge that fingerprints help solve crimes has also prompted individuals to wear gloves while they commit crimes to make an effort to wipe away the telltale evidence. What criminals may not know is that gloves with textured finger surfaces can themselves be identified. This is because the finger surface texturing is typically random in pattern, meaning that the pattern will not be exactly the same for another finger on that glove or for another glove, as with fingerprints. If the gloves are found in the possession of a suspect and the glove prints can be identified to a particular finger of a glove, this situation can actually be more incriminating than the presence of fingerprints, because it shows intent to cover up the crime on the part of the defendant.

Likewise, wipe marks can tell a tale. Suppose a person wipes down a gun or the inside of a vehicle in an effort to destroy any prints inadvertently left behind. Even though no fingerprints can be developed, the wipe marks are usually visible when fingerprint powder or superglue fuming is used on the surface. Sometimes a fabric pattern is left, and a fabric pattern can, in rare cases, point to a particular type cloth that was used. If a suspect happens to have such a cloth in his or her possession, that provides circumstantial evidence.

In conclusion, fingerprints can and do play a vital role in the reconstruction of crimes. Finding fingerprints on weapons, especially when there is no legitimate explanation for their presence, essentially puts the weapon in the perpetrator's hands. Unfortunately, however, there is no scientifically valid means of establishing when fingerprints were deposited on a surface. Studies, as well as casework, have shown that fingerprints left on surfaces years earlier can still be found. Thus, defendants can argue that fingerprints were left long before the crime. This argument goes by the wayside when there is no legitimate reason for their fingerprints to be present at all.

The case study that follows illustrates how the combination of fingerprint identification and firearms examinations work together to facilitate the reconstruction of a crime. This case is especially interesting from the fingerprint standpoint because it is a rare example of identifiable fingerprints being present on a firearm. The firearms aspects that this case will illustrate include bullet and cartridge case identification to a specific weapon as well as trajectory analysis and gunshot residue testing. The implications of criminal investigative efforts are also illustrated.

The reconstruction of a crime must consider the implications of information derived from the investigative efforts of the lead officer in a criminal investigation along with the results of field and laboratory testing relating to the physical evidence. It is important, for example, for the individual who is reconstructing a shooting incident to have any information that might establish a motive. Without a motive for homicide or suicide the evaluation of a possible accidental shooting takes on added importance. On the other hand a clear motive for homicide gives the examiner an initial area of concentration with regard to the physical evidence. All this must be tempered with extreme care to avoid "tunnel vision" and jumping to conclusions.

## A DOUBLE HOMICIDE IN ARIZONA

In the late 1990s an East Indian couple purchased a rundown truck stop/café on Interstate 40 between Flagstaff and Kingman, Arizona. They planned to modernize and improve the establishment and hoped to turn it into a successful business. At the time of the purchase the business had three employees: a diesel mechanic, a cook, and a waitress who was the cook's longtime girlfriend.

It soon became apparent to the new owners that the cook and the waitress were not a good match with their new business. Both were obviously resentful of the changes the new owners had announced. Furthermore, the owners suspected the waitress of theft and prostitution. They informed the cook and the waitress that their services would no longer be needed after the end of the month, 10 days away. The diesel mechanic, who lived behind the café in a trailer, seemed reliable and trustworthy, and the new owners proposed to keep him on in this capacity.

The day before the cook and waitress were supposed to leave, the 911 dispatcher at the Coconino County Sheriff's Office received a call reporting an apparent robbery and double homicide at the truck stop. The call was made by the cook. When officers arrived, the cook told them that he had been out back emptying the trash when he heard "two loud bangs" from inside the truck stop. As he rushed in through the side door, he said he discovered the owner lying on the floor bleeding profusely from gunshot wounds to the head. The owner's wife was slumped over in a nearby booth, also bleeding from an apparent gunshot wound to the left cheek. There was blood on the floor and on a partition wall between the dining area and the kitchen. The cash drawer was open, and all the money was gone. The cook stated that as he looked out the front window of the café, he saw two white males speeding away to the west in a red compact pickup.

Police dispatched the highway patrol, which spotted a red Toyota pickup with two white males headed west on I-40. A police helicopter caught up with the vehicle and by loudspeaker ordered the driver to pull over, but instead the truck pulled onto a side road. This action, of course, convinced the officer's that they had the murderers in their sight. Actually, the driver and passenger in the pickup were on their way from Texas to California in search of employment and sharing a marijuana cigarette to pass the time. Not wishing to be caught with the marijuana—and in their dulled state of awareness—the two decided to attempt to evade the helicopter by taking a side road off the interstate.

After several menacing dives from the helicopter, the young men decided to stop and give up, having long since tossed out the contraband. To their surprise they soon learned they had far greater problems than driving while under the influence of a controlled substance. After hours of interrogation and the pair's steadfast denial of any involvement in the murders, a break came back at the crime scene.

An investigator searching the area behind the truck stop noticed a pile of rocks. Exposed areas of fresh dirt and debris suggested that several rocks had been recently replaced. Upon removing the rocks the officer discovered a small semiautomatic pistol. Officers delivered the pistol to the crime laboratory and asked the lab to process it for latent prints. Once autopsies were complete, the pistol was to be compared to bullets recovered from the victims.

At the crime laboratory latent print unit, a visual inspection turned up no fingerprints, so the examiner used superglue fuming in an effort to develop any latent prints. Unexpectedly, a very good quality fingerprint was found on the pistol. The examiner applied charcoal powder over the superglue to enhance the fingerprint, scanned the fingerprint, and put it into an AFIS. To everyone's surprise a "hit" was made. The latent fingerprint matched a file fingerprint for the cook, who had a previous arrest record for petty theft and aggravated assault.

At this point the police released the two young men, somewhat the worse for wear, and they headed on to California vowing never to smoke marijuana again. The focus of the investigation turned to the cook. The cook acknowledged that he was dismissed at the end of the month but insisted that it did not bother him. He had simply planned to take his girlfriend and move on. Even when confronted with the fact that his fingerprint had been found on what had been confirmed as the murder weapon, he refused to admit any involvement.

The pistol, it turned out, belonged to the diesel mechanic. When first interviewed, the mechanic readily admitted that he owned a pistol. He said that he kept the pistol in a drawer in the shop, but when he took officers out there to retrieve it, it was missing. He said that he and the cook had occasionally shot the pistol while in the back of the truck stop. He also said that the cook knew about the drawer where the pistol was kept.

At this point investigators decided to reconstruct the shooting in an attempt to shed some light on exactly how the shooting took place. A review of the autopsy report provided some important information. According to the autopsy report,

- The man was shot once in the right side of the neck (a bullet was recovered from the left side of his neck) with the bullet traveling at a downward angle of approximately 30 degrees.

- The man was also shot in the top of the head with the bullet exiting under his chin (a bullet was recovered on the floor in the pool of blood the man was lying in).

- The woman was shot once in the left cheek, the bullet striking her brain stem causing her to collapse where she sat in the booth and killing her instantly (a bullet was recovered from her neck).

- The bullet that struck her was traveling at a downward angle of approximately 20 degrees.

- No gunshot residue or powder stippling was found around the wounds in either victim.

Additional information useful for reconstructing the shooting was obtained from the crime scene report. According to the crime scene report,

- The cash register drawer was open, and all the money was gone.

- All the fired cartridge cases were in the immediate area of the two victims.

- There was a trail of blood drops leading from the booth where the female was found to the location of the male victim's body.

- There were no footwear impressions in the blood trail.

- There was a V-shaped bloodstain pattern on top of the partial wall next to the booth the female victim was in.

- No other similar V patterns were observed.

- No blood was found on the table in the booth.

- A bullet was found embedded in the floor close to the male victim's right hand.

- There was a pattern of projected blood from the pool the male victim's head was lying in.

- A crime scene diagram was prepared to show the locations of the victims and some of the bloodstains.

According to the crime laboratory results,

- The pistol found behind the truck stop fired all the bullets and cartridge cases found.

- The pistol and ammunition failed to deposit gunshot residue on targets 30 inches (76.2 cm) or more from the muzzle of the gun.

- The V-shaped bloodstain was from the man.

- Only the man's blood was found in the floor stains.

The cook had said that after hearing "two loud bangs" he came in through the back door and ran to the front counter. But how did he get past the male victim's body (V2) that was partially blocking the way, and how did he get across the bloodstains on the floor without stepping in them? The answer was obvious: He was lying about his movements. When the cook was confronted with this finding, he refused to talk any further.

According to the crime scene diagram, there were two chairs at the table directly across from the female victim (V1). The one closest to the partial wall is pushed in, while the other one is out from the table. In reconstructing the shooting all these bits of information are important.

The easy part of this reconstruction is determining the position of the female victim when she was shot. Since her brain stem was struck by the bullet that entered her left cheek, there would have been no way for her to move from her original position. Clearly she was seated in the booth when she was shot. The downward trajectory of the bullet that struck her indicated that the shooter was holding the gun above her (that is, probably standing upright).

The V-shaped bloodstain was indicative of an arterial spurt. The blood was identified as coming from the male. The shot to the man's right neck had severed an artery. Once that happened, blood would have spurted with each beat of his heart until pressure was lost. But the man was shot in the right side of the neck, and there were no more similar patterns present.

The man presented a greater threat than the woman, and on that basis alone it is reasonable to expect that he was shot first. Since he could not have been seated, gotten shot in the neck, and gotten up all before his heart beat and produced the V pattern arterial spurt, he had to have been standing. The location of the blood indicated that he was standing behind the pushed in chair.

Once a person is shot, the individual frequently presses his or her hands against the wound(s) to stop or slow the flow of blood. That is doubtless why no additional arterial spurts were present in the crime scene. With his right hand pressed against the wound in his right neck, blood probably began to run down his arm and drip off his right elbow as he slowly moved toward the back room. He stopped briefly in the doorway, slipped in his own blood before turning back toward the front room, and fell forward where he was found.

The fact that the bullet to the back of the man's head exited under his chin and was found in the pool of blood his head was lying in meant that he had to have been shot in that position. The bullet found in the floor next to the man's right hand indicated that a shot was fired that had missed. The question that needed to be answered here was which of these two shots was fired first? By determining the angle at which the bullet struck the floor, it was possible to establish the approximate distance the cook would have been when this shot was fired. That turned out to be about 12 feet (3.7 m). Doing the same kind of analysis for the shot to the top of the man's head resulted in a distance of approximately four feet (1.2 m) away for the cook.

Common sense would suggest that if a shot was fired from 12 feet (3.7 m) and missed, the next shot would be fired from a closer range. Hence, the shot to the back of the head was likely the last shot fired and the shot into the floor the next to last.

Pursuant to summarizing all of this information following is the probable sequence of events:

1. The woman was seated in the booth talking to her husband, who was standing across from her at the north side of the booth table.

2. The cook came to the south side of the booth, drew a pistol, and shot the man in the right side of the neck.

3. As the man staggered away toward the back room, the cook turned the gun on the man's wife, shooting her in the left side of the face and killing her instantly.

4. The cook then went to the cash register, opened it, and took the money to make it appear that a robbery had been committed,

5. He then looked out the front window, saw a red pickup driving by with two white males in it, called 911, and reported a robbery-murder, describing the red truck as "leaving the scene."

6. At some point, either before or after the 911 call, the male victim must have attempted to get up off the floor.

7. Seeing the man was still alive, the cook shot at him and missed.

8. The cook then moved within a few feet of the man and shot him in the top of the head execution style.

9. The cook then went out back, hid the gun, and waited for officers to arrive.

Whenever a reconstruction such as this is done, one must always let the facts direct the course of actions while relying on experience and training that relates to the event. The reconstruction that results is nothing more than a probable or likely sequence of events based on all these things. The individuals involved in the reconstruction or otherwise impacted by the outcome always must wonder how close to the actual event the reconstruction comes.

In this particular case a rare glimpse at the actual event was provided to investigators after the reconstruction had been completed. This was because the cook's common-law wife, who was working as a waitress in the truck stop, finally agreed to tell the truth about the shootings in exchange for immunity from prosecution. Initially she had claimed to have been in the kitchen when the shots were fired and "didn't see a thing." When prosecutors informed her that she was going to be charged with being an accessory to murder if she did not tell the truth, she changed her tune. She could not, however, be compelled to testify in court against her common-law husband, and she elected not to do so.

The story she ultimately told paralleled the reconstruction with remarkable accuracy. She stated that she had been seated in the chair at the south end of the table at the booth directly across from the female. She said the male was standing to her left, leaning over the table talking, when her husband walked up, pulled a gun, and shot the male and then the female.

The cook then went to the cash register, removed the money, and gave it to her to put in her purse. The cook saw the red truck driving by and called 911, reported the shooting, and described the truck and its occupants to the police. Once he got off the phone, the cook saw the male victim trying to get up off the floor. The cook walked over next to the booth where the female was collapsed and fired at the man but missed. He then walked up closer and shot the man in the top of the head. The cook then went outside and said he was getting rid of the gun.

The end result here was that the reconstruction of the shooting had been right on the money. Certainly some of the events could have differed in sequence, but by taking a logical approach to the significance of the evidence and being conservative with opinions related to it, it is usually possible for the investigator to be on pretty safe ground, as was the case here.

## SHOTS FIRED AT A MOVING VEHICLE
## KILL THE YOUNG DRIVER

Shooting incident reconstruction involves a variety of factors. It is not uncommon for moving vehicles to be part of shooting incidents. Additional considerations are involved when the target is moving, the shooter is moving, or both are moving. In this case the shooter was stationary, and the target, the driver of a Jeep, was moving.

This shooting incident took place in a rural area of a western state known for its "survivalist types" and armed militia. Three teens were riding around in an open Jeep in a sparsely populated area. They were drinking as they drove and were causing the Jeep to backfire by switching the ignition switch on and off. It was approaching sundown as they turned down a narrow stretch of road that led past a small frame house that was essentially surrounded by foliage and underbrush. Only about a 30-foot opening directly across the front allowed a passerby any sort of view of the house and grounds from the roadway.

As they approached the opening in the foliage, they caused the jeep to backfire one more time. Just as they drove past the opening, the driver suddenly slumped forward in the seat. The Jeep, now out of control, crossed over to the left and collided with a pickup parked on the side of the road. With the radio of the Jeep blaring and the intermittent backfires, the other two teens in the vehicle had heard nothing and had no idea what had happened until they saw a wound on the left side of the driver's head with blood running out.

Police officers interviewed the owner of the house that the incident had taken place in front of. He stated that he had been out in front of his house with a 22-caliber rifle "hunting skunks" when he heard the sound of the approaching vehicle. As the vehicle got close, he said that he heard what he thought was a gunshot and instinctively "hit the deck" while holding the rifle up so as not to strike the ground. He said that when he did that, his right thumb was in the trigger guard, and he "may have accidentally fired a shot." When he showed the officers where this took place, a single fired 22-cartridge case was found on the ground. The crime scene is shown in the diagram.

Ultimately officers determined that the Jeep had what appeared to be a recent bullet hole in the rocker molding below the driver side door opening. A search of the roadway failed to locate a fired bullet. It was

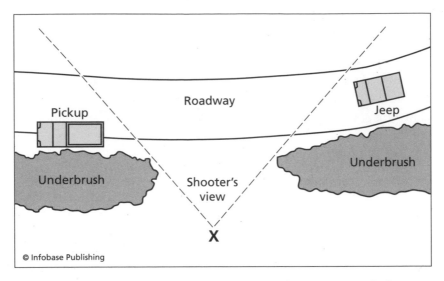

Crime scene diagram from a shooting incident involving a motor vehicle

also noted that the left rear tire of the Jeep was flat. The tire was removed from the rim and a small piece of nondescript lead was found inside. This piece of lead was about the right weight for a 22-caliber bullet but had no visible bullet characteristics, such as rifling marks or copper coating. A search warrant was obtained, and the rifle was seized from the man, together with a partial box of 22 long rifle cartridges from inside the house.

The question that had to be answered was whether there had been only one shot, as suggested by the single cartridge case, or multiple shots, as suggested by the hole in the rocker molding and the piece of lead in the left rear tire. To help answer this investigators shipped the bullet removed from the boy's head at autopsy, the cartridges from the man's residence, and the piece of lead to the FBI laboratory in Washington, D.C., for elemental analysis. Elemental analysis provides a means of determining the exact makeup of a substance in terms of what is present and in what quantity. This was necessary to determine whether the lead fragment from the tire was, in fact, a bullet or a piece of lead wheel weight (something that occasionally ends up inside tires when they have been remounted). Equally important was to establish whether the three samples could have come from the same lot of ammunition.

Lead bullets, such as in many types of 22 long rifle cartridges, consist not only of lead but also have tin and sometimes antimony as part of their formulation. That is done to make the bullets harder so that they have less of a tendency to distort on impact. Elemental analysis is used to determine which of the chemical elements are present and what their percentage composition is. Once the FBI analysis was complete, a report was issued indicating that all three samples were similar in composition and came from the same lot of ammunition.

The term *lot of ammunition* refers to a production run. In this age of computer-controlled manufacturing, variations in formulations are much less pronounced than they used to be; however, it is still possible to find measurable differences in the compositions from lot to lot. The FBI finding was huge. Three shots, not one, were indicated. While it may have been possible for the man to accidentally fire one round as he hit the ground, the firing of three shots could simply not have taken place by accident. Particularly since the shots were confined to a rather small area of the moving target. At this juncture investigators decided that a reconstruction was in order. The questions that needed answering included the following:

- Where did the shots come from? Near the ground or from some other position, such as with the shooter standing upright?

- Was it possible for three shots to have been fired as the Jeep passed by the opening in the foliage in front of the house?

- Would the rifle hit what it was aimed at?

- How would the rifle have been manipulated in order to hit the boy once and the Jeep twice?

The most reliable indicator of shooter position was the bullet hole through the driver door rocker molding. That is because it was a fixed object on the Jeep, whereas the driver's exact position could never be determined nor could the position of the tire when the bullet struck it. Of course, the Jeep could have been situated on the road in a number of positions when the shot struck the molding. What had to be done was to try positioning the Jeep at various positions (that is, to the far right side, middle, and far left side of the one-lane road) and tracing the trajectory back to the location the man said he had hit the ground at. If the resultant trajectories were the same, the position of the Jeep on the road would be a moot point. If different positions yielded drastically differing points of origin, the situation would become complicated, and resolution would be necessary.

Rather than take the Jeep back to the scene and try to move it about, it was decided to construct a mock-up that incorporated the molding such that it was at the same height above the ground as it originally was when affixed to the Jeep. The mock-up was light and portable so that it was easy to move about on the roadway to do trajectory analysis. The mock-up also permitted the use of a laser that was projected through the bullet hole from the inside of the molding. The laser beam represented the bullet trajectory and allowed quick determinations to be made as to the probable shooter position for the various positions of the Jeep on the roadway. The results were the same for every possible position of the Jeep: The shot came from a position close to the ground in the area the man had identified. Did that mean he was telling the truth?

Even though the shot to the molding was consistent with coming from close to the ground, as the man had stated, the problem was the other two shots and the moving target. As already pointed out, there was simply no way that three shots could have accidentally hit the driver and the Jeep, the main reason being that in order for the shots to strike the moving target, the gun barrel would have had to follow or track the Jeep and its occupants. In order to quantify this it would be necessary to know how fast the Jeep was moving as it came into view from the man's position. By knowing how fast the Jeep was going and what the field of view of the target was from the man's position, it could be determined how long the Jeep remained in view. Once that was determined, it would be necessary to know how fast the weapon could be fired (that is, Could three shots have been fired in the time frame the target was visible?).

A good estimate of the Jeep's speed was obtained by examination of the damage that resulted from impact with the parked vehicle following the shooting. Using the principles of accident reconstruction and the associated formulas for calculating speed at impact based upon vehicle damage, it was determined that the Jeep was going approximately 25 miles per hour (40.2 kph). Interviews with the two passengers in the Jeep corroborated that approximate speed.

The "window of opportunity" for the shooter was determined by measuring the opening in the underbrush along the roadway through which the shots had to have come. This was found to be approximately 30 feet (9.1 m). Using the speed of 25 mph, the time required for the Jeep to traverse the 30-foot view that the shooter had of the Jeep was determined to be 0.8 second. The calculations are summarized below:

Conversion of miles (km)/hour to feet (m)/second:
25 miles (40.2 km)/hour × 1 hour/3,600 seconds × 5,280 feet (1,609.3 m)/mile (1.6 km) = 36.6 feet (11.2 m)/second

Calculation of time required to travel 30 feet (9.1 m):
30 feet (9.1 m) ÷ 36.6 feet (11.2 m)/second = 0.8 second

The remaining task was to determine how fast the semiautomatic 22 rifle could be fired. This was somewhat subjective since it would obviously not be a question limited to mechanical function alone: Different people would probably differ somewhat in how rapidly they could fire a given weapon. The first thought might be to have the man show how fast he could fire the weapon. However, the pitfall associated with that sort of experiment was brought home in the O. J. Simpson case when the prosecution asked Simpson to try on the glove in front of the jury, and he had a great deal of "difficulty," leaving the impression that it did not fit and producing the outcry on the part of some "If the glove doesn't fit, you must acquit."

The best that could be done was to establish the maximum rate of fire for the weapon and leave it at that. Doing that resulted in a maximum rate of fire of four shots per second. The answer as to whether three shots could have been fired at the Jeep and its occupants from the man's position as the Jeep passed by was found through one more calculation.

Calculation of the number of shots possible in 0.8 second:
0.8 second × 4 shots/second = 3.2 shots

It was therefore possible for three shots to have been fired in the time allotted. The tracking that was required for the shots to strike the Jeep and driver was particularly incriminating and indicated intent. At trial the fact that only one fired cartridge case was present at the scene was used by the prosecution to show that the man had not only intentionally fired the shots but had then tried to cover up his crime by removing two fired cartridge cases and leaving the one. It was believed that the man probably did not know that he had hit the rocker molding and the tire in addition to hitting the driver.

One question that is begged is what possible motivation was there for the shooting. It was learned that the kids had been in that area before and had had a previous run-in with the man. The man had apparently been so angered by the first encounter that he had set out to get revenge should they ever return. It was their bad fortune to do so. The man was convicted of first-degree murder and sentenced to life in prison. Had he not have hit the molding and the tire, as well as the driver, he might have well gotten away with murder, as it would have been extremely difficult to prove it was not an accident as he had described.

This case illustrates some of the varied aspects of shooting incident reconstruction that can arise from the particular circumstances of a shooting. It also illustrates the need for a firearms examiner to be creative and adaptable in the process of reconstructing a crime. Above all, the examiner must be observant and detail oriented in order to be able to carry out the reconstruction of a crime. A further example of the application of these skills is found in the following two case studies.

## A STAGED CRIME SCENE IS UNCOVERED BY INVESTIGATORS

In this case the careful inspection of the victim and the crime scene by the firearms examiner and the latent print examiner revealed that the crime scene had been staged. Such observations are the product of training, experience, and individual skills of perception. Training and experience can be had by anyone; perceptive skills are another matter. Analogous to athletic ability, either you have it or you do not. Basic innate abilities can be honed and developed, but that can only go so far. Thus, top-notch crime scene investigators are born, not made.

A call came in to 911 by a woman stating that she had just shot her husband as he attacked her with a knife. Officers arrived to find a

The body *(Courtesy of the author)*

man lying face down in a pool of blood in a hallway, a knife clutched in his right hand. The man, as it turned out, had moved out several weeks earlier after his wife announced that she had a lesbian lover. The couple had a 12-year-old daughter who had continued to live at the home with the mother and her new companion, much to the father's dismay.

The father reportedly grew so distraught over his daughter being in what he considered to be an unacceptable environment that he showed up that day demanding that his daughter leave with him. According to the wife, a heated argument had ensued in which the husband came into her bedroom armed with a butcher knife and attacked her. She said that she grabbed a pistol from the nightstand and shot him in the chest just as he lunged for her. Upon being shot, she said, he "clutched his chest with both hands, turned and staggered out into the hallway where he collapsed." She said that she had not touched the body.

The crime scene investigation was carried out with the assistance of a firearms examiner and a latent print examiner. The crime scene

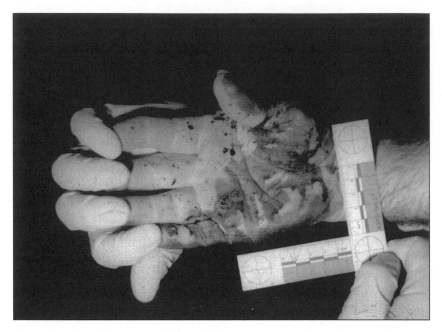

The victim's hand *(Courtesy of the author)*

investigator had asked for their assistance shortly after arriving at the scene and making an initial evaluation. The crime scene investigator had become suspicious of the woman's story after viewing the husband's body and the area around it. In particular, the fact that the knife was still in the husband's right hand raised a big question in the investigator's mind. The woman had said that he grabbed his chest with both hands after she shot him. How could he do that and still have the knife in his hand? Also, why would he continue to hold the knife as he moved out of the bedroom and into the hall, and how could he have fallen to the floor and never let go of the knife?

The answers to these questions were provided by the latent print examiner after an examination of the husband's right hand and an examination of the knife was conducted. It can be seen in the accompanying photographs that the palm of the husband's right hand was covered with blood such that blood should have been transferred to the handle of the knife. But an examination of the knife handle showed almost no blood, as can be seen in the other photograph.

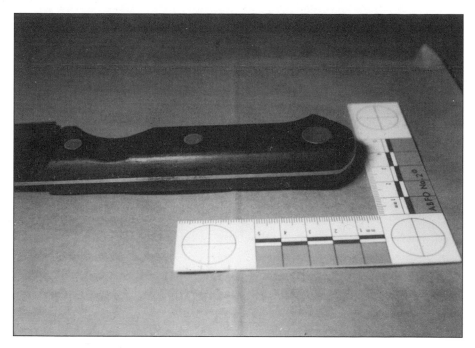

The knife *(Courtesy of the author)*

Another look at the palm of the husband's right hand revealed specks of blood that could only have landed on the palm if the knife were not present. Clearly the woman was lying about the knife. A check of the kitchen revealed that there was a butcher-block holder with similar knives. Looking again at the area between the wall and the husband's right arm, investigators could see that the bloodstains indicated that the man's right arm had been back near his body with his hands together against the wall.

Putting all this together, it became clear that the woman had pulled the man's right arm away from his body as he lay on the floor after dying and placed the knife in his hand. Since the blood had not been transferred to the knife handle from the palm of his hand, there had been sufficient passage of time for the blood to dry. This indicated that she must have decided to stage the crime scene a half-hour or so after she had shot him. When confronted with this evidence, she continued to deny it; however, her daughter admitted the ruse. The woman was convicted of murder. Her attempt to cover up the crime weighed heavily against her at trial.

## HOMICIDE OR SUICIDE? AN UNUSUAL CASE THAT LEAVES INVESTIGATORS PUZZLED

One of the most frequently encountered questions that investigators must answer is whether homicide or suicide is the cause of a shooting death. Many times there are indicators of both, making the call very difficult. Following is just such a case. It began with a 911 call from a male voice identifying himself as the victim and stating, "I've just accidentally shot myself." Upon arrival responding officers found the man lying on the bedroom floor dressed in pants but no shirt and shot in the right side of his chest. Gunpowder stippling was clearly visible in a six-inch (15.2-cm) circular pattern around the wound.

Upon rolling the man's body over, officers observed an apparent exit wound in the man's lower back. The exit wound was determined to be approximately four inches (10.2 cm) below the height of the entry wound, as measured from the bottom of the man's feet. A Ruger Single-Six revolver was lying on the floor not far from the man's feet.

The hammer was down on a fired cartridge case. There was another fired cartridge case next to the first. There were four live rounds in the cylinder. The firearms examiner who was called to the scene to assist recognized that, based on the rotation direction of the cylinder, the cartridge case not under the hammer would have been fired first.

Further examination of the scene revealed a bullet hole in the ceiling above the location of the body. The telephone was observed to be off its cradle and lying on a nightstand next to the bed.

Based upon the bullet hole in the ceiling and the exit wound being lower than the entrance wound, it appeared that the man was shot while bent over at the waist with the gun barrel below his chest and pointing upward. But did that necessarily mean homicide and not suicide? What about an accidental shooting? After all, the caller had said, "I've just accidentally shot myself"?

In order to be able to rule in or rule out a self-inflicted gunshot, either suicide or accidental, it was necessary to establish the

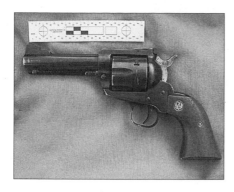

The weapon
(Courtesy of the author)

approximate distance of the shot. This was possible due to the fact that there was a pattern of gunpowder stippling around the wound. The firearms examiner took the revolver and ammunition like that found in the gun and carried out test firings to duplicate the six-inch stippling pattern on the victim. The results indicated a shot between 12 and 24 inches (30.5 cm and 61 cm) from the body. Since this was within arm's length, a self-inflicted gunshot could not be eliminated.

A check of the revolver and ammunition had failed to produce any identifiable fingerprints. No check was made of the house itself, leaving the question open as to whether there had been an intruder, but there was no sign of forced entry or anything else to suggest that another person had been present at the time of the shooting.

Anytime the question of possible suicide comes up, it is necessary to determine if a possible motive for suicide exists. Things that are commonly linked to suicide include health problems, financial problems, and loss of loved ones. In this case none of those possibilities existed. For murder to be a consideration there would have to be a suspect with a motive and the opportunity to commit the act. Again investigators hit a brick wall. Neither suicide nor homicide could be ruled out with 100 percent certainty.

Some interesting evidence resulted from the autopsy of the victim. Linear soot deposits were observed in the palms of the victim's hands. There was also powder stippling on the inside of the victim's right arm, several inches above the wrist. Whenever linear soot deposits are found on a shooting victim and a revolver is involved, cylinder gap deposits are the most likely source. The gap between the front of the

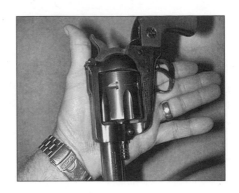

Position of the right hand
(*Courtesy of the author*)

chamber and the barrel allows gases from the burning gunpowder to escape to both sides of the weapon. This results in the deposition of soot on anything in close proximity. Typically the soot deposition will be linear in appearance.

If the hand were placed over the side of a revolver and the revolver discharged, a linear soot pattern would be expected. A simulation of how the gun would have been oriented with respect to the left hand is seen in the figures.

The fact that linear soot deposits were also present in the palm of the victim's left hand meant that it, too, was in contact with the cylinder gap area. The positions of both hands are depicted in the following figure. The question of homicide or suicide could not, however, be answered on this alone. Certainly the fact that both hands had to be grasping the gun was more suggestive of homicide than suicide, but holding the gun in that manner still permitted firing by using one or both forefingers. The bullet hole in the ceiling and the trajectory of the bullet through the body certainly did not suggest suicide, but what about the 911 call? The question that had to be answered was whose voice was that? Unfortunately by the time investigators thought about that, the tape had been erased. There was then no way to verify that the victim was really the caller.

There was still the consideration that the shot was accidental, just as the call had stated. After all, there was no apparent motive for either suicide or homicide. The firearms examiner had pointed out that the gun could only be fired when the hammer was fully cocked and the trigger pulled. It could not fire as a result of falling and hitting the

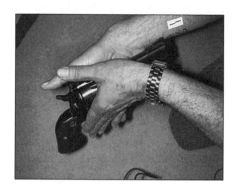

Gun in both hands
*(Courtesy of the author)*

floor. If it was accidental, then the victim had to have been handling it with the hammer cocked—not a very wise thing to do, for sure.

The investigator decided to test the accidental theory by cocking the weapon, holding it in the manner indicated by the soot deposits, then bending over with the arms extended as if the gun was falling to the floor and he was grabbing for it. As the butt of the gun made contact with floor, he found his forefinger could go against the trigger hard enough to make the hammer fall. Thus, accidental firing could not be ruled out.

At this stage the investigator has to look at which of the three possible scenarios is most probable. In addition to the lack of motive for suicide, the fact that the shot entered the lower right chest made suicide a very unlikely prospect. There being no evidence to support homicide other than the position of the hands around the gun, the only option left was accidental. The fact that testing indicated that the weapon could be unintentionally discharged, coupled with the content of the 911 call, verifiable or not, left accidental as the most likely cause. Was that what actually happened? Most likely we will never know.

Crime scene reconstruction relies heavily on the physical evidence left at the scene. For firearms evidence the function testing of weapons, bullet and cartridge case examinations and comparisons, gunshot residue analysis, and trajectory analysis are areas that are frequently involved. Fingerprint evidence can specifically place a suspect at a crime scene. Various methods of physical and chemical means are available to the examiner for the development of fingerprints. Additionally, useful information that can assist in the reconstruction is obtained through the criminal investigative efforts. The combination of the physical evidence test results and the results of the criminal investigation lead to the proposal of a probable scenario for crime.

5

# The Future

The field of forensic science, like other areas of science, is continuously changing with the introduction of new technologies. The application of technology designed for one area to another unrelated area is becoming more the rule than the exception. What is today's high-tech achievement is tomorrow's routine procedure. Technology related to firearms and fingerprints is no different. This final chapter will explore some of the emerging technology associated with these two disciplines and set the stage for what the future may hold.

## FINGERPRINTS AND DNA

The traditional approach to personal identification has been to examine an object for the presence of identifiable fingerprints, enhancing vague or partial prints as appropriate. With the advent of AFIS the next hurdle for the fingerprint examiner was to ensure that the fingerprints be of "AFIS quality." This allows the fingerprints to be entered into an AFIS and searched against the database. If the fingerprints are deemed not to be of appropriate quality, the AFIS search cannot be made. This means

that the fingerprints can only be compared directly to fingerprints of known suspects, eliminating the ability to utilize the AFIS database to locate unknown suspects.

The DNA in fingerprint residues offers the potential to change all of that. Since fingerprints are partly composed of protein residues, it is possible to extract DNA from a fingerprint. The DNA may then be used to identify an individual even when the fingerprints themselves are

## Firearms, Fingerprints, and DNA

An off-duty federal agent was the victim of a carjacking. The carjacker disarmed the agent and turned his own gun on him. The agent was shot to death and the gun left at the scene, near his body. His vehicle, which had been stripped of its wheels and stereo, was discovered several days later near a housing project. A suspect was determined to be residing in the project.

The vehicle was carefully examined for hairs, fibers, and other trace evidence, but none was found. There were no visible fingerprints on the steering wheel, and because it had a textured surface, investigators deemed it unlikely to retain identifiable fingerprints. Furthermore, the chemicals needed to enhance the fingerprints would probably destroy any DNA that might be present. As a result, they decided to forgo fingerprinting on the steering wheel and conduct DNA testing instead.

A similar decision was made regarding the dead agent's gun, a Glock semiautomatic pistol. Its surfaces were also textured and unlikely to have identifiable fingerprints present, so investigators took swabs off the outer surfaces of the frame, slide, and trigger. Since there was no reason to suspect that the killer had handled the magazine and remaining ammunition inside, these items were not swabbed for DNA.

DNA analysis of the swabs from the gun failed to produce identifiable DNA. The swabs from the steering wheel, however, recorded DNA that was a mixture of the dead agent and the suspect. On the basis of this analysis, the suspect was convicted of the crime and sentenced to death.

inadequate for identification. This technology has even been applied to fingerprints lifted with tape at crime scenes: The tape has been pulled from its viewing card and the DNA extracted from the residue.

Rather than further limiting the usability of fingerprints, as AFIS has done to some degree by stepping up the quality requirements, DNA analysis works just as well on smudges and smears as on clear fingerprints. In fact, smudges and smears may be better suited to DNA analysis due to increased contact between the surface and the finger, thus resulting in the transfer of more DNA-containing material. This means that fingerprints that cannot otherwise be identified because they are smeared, incomplete, or otherwise lack adequate detail may still be useful as evidence.

## THE EYES MAY HAVE IT

As far back as the 1930s, in the context of biometric research, people recognized that the blood vessels at the back of the eye might be unique in pattern and offer a means of individual identification. Retinal scanning technology has been around as an alternative means for personal identification since the mid-1970s. Retinal scanning analyzes the layer of blood vessels at the very back of the eye. These blood vessels form a pattern that is totally random and unique, just like fingerprints. Tales abound about various uses of dead people's fingers being used to falsify fingerprints as though the individual were still alive. There is no known way to replicate a retina, however, and the retina of a dead person would deteriorate rapidly, eliminating the need to prove the retina is from a live person.

Retinal scanning involves the use of a low-intensity light and an optical coupler to read the blood vessel patterns. There is a certain amount of discomfort in that the individual who is being scanned must focus on a particular point within the optics of the scanner and remain focused for approximately 10 seconds. Naturally, those who wear glasses have to remove them for the scanning.

Minimal discomfort aside, retinal scanning has been used almost exclusively in high-risk security areas such as military installations. The state of Illinois uses retinal scans to prevent welfare fraud. The Japanese use retinal scans at automated teller machines.

New uses appear to be on the horizon. For instance, media reports have indicated that retinal scans are being considered for student identification. This is due to their accuracy and mobility; obviously, there is no real concern that students will be likely to bring in dead fingers to attempt to falsify their true identity. Advantages include eliminating the social stigma associated with certain programs such as receiving free lunch at school. By giving everyone a retinal scan, the haves could be distinguished from the have-nots in an unobtrusive manner. The device could also be used in the library and at social events to keep outsiders away. Similarly test takers could be verified as to identity quickly and easily; no more paid test takers for college or graduate school entrance exams.

One problem with retinal scans is that the retina changes over time. This necessitates periodic updates to the database to keep the scanning current. As an alternative to retinal scans the iris of the eye has been used. The iris does not change. Iris scans video the colored area of the eye and record the unique pattern present. Iris scanning allows the individual being scanned to be as far as several feet away from the device. Obviously, cataracts and lens replacement surgeries would have to be considered, but these conditions affect a relatively small proportion of the population.

Alternatives to retinal scanning include fingerprint scanners, which are in use around the world. These rely on a template being created with the first scan. All subsequent scans are compared against the template on file. To eliminate the possibility of a fake or dead finger, infrared light can be used to verify that there is a pulse within the finger itself.

According to an April 12, 2004, article in *Business Week,* experts at the University of Leicester have developed a high-speed identification system based on the shape and features of the ear. A preliminary study of 1,500 ears has shown that no two ears are identical. The study did not mention whether identical twins were part of the group. If the ear is unique, it would be expected that the ears of "identical" twins would be different.

The progression from fingerprints to other physical characteristics for purposes of individual identification speaks to ongoing efforts to come up with a simple, direct method that defies compromise. Retinal scan appears to be the most likely candidate. Of course, the possibility of someone wearing contact lenses that display the retinal pattern of another individual comes to mind. That may be a meaningless concern, but criminal minds sometimes come up with ingenious ways to "beat the system."

## FIREARMS THAT CAN "TALK"

For years firearms safety advocates have wished that there were some way for firearms to be able to communicate with their owners such that they would recognize whether the individual who was attempting to fire them was authorized. Certainly combination locks on triggers represent a step in this direction. More sophisticated devices such as fingerprint or retinal scanners are too bulky and expensive in their current configurations, but what if they could be miniaturized?

The need for instant shooter recognition is found in police and personal safety situations. Police officers being disarmed and shot with their own weapons has been an unfortunate issue since the inception of armed police departments. A firearm that could instantly recognize that the designated officer was not holding the weapon could prevent such happenings. Likewise, this would be beneficial to private individuals who confront assailants and are disarmed and their firearms used against them.

After a weapon is fired, investigators often must try to determine whether a particular spent bullet or casing was discharged from a particular firearm. Firearms examiners have long wished that firearms could impart some sort of identifier to ammunition, above and beyond the traditional tool marks that are left. For instance, an implanted device would provide some sort of electronic fingerprint for both the ammunition components and the firearm. As yet, however, all these ideas remain within the realm of science fiction.

## PHANTOM FIREARMS

Certain firearms create real problems for the forensic firearms examiner, and such firearms are under development. Consider cartridge cases. During the Civil War era caseless ammunition was the norm. Instead of brass cartridge cases, gunpowder was contained in paper packets. Since there was no metallic cartridge case, there was, of course, nothing for the various markings traditionally produced by firing to appear on. With the development of metallic cartridge cases in the 1850s came the potential for identification of firearms from the markings left by firing pins, chambers, breech faces, extractors, ejectors, and magazines during discharge.

History seems to be repeating itself. Caseless cartridges are once more the fancy of the shooting world. This is due mainly to the economy associated with not having a metallic cartridge case. Instead, epoxy-bonded powder charges with integral primers are affixed to bullets, eliminating the need for metallic cartridge cases. The problem for the firearms examiner in criminal investigations is apparent.

Yet another "phantom" is the development of firearms with electronic ignition of priming mixtures. Rather than having a firing pin to ignite the primer, these weapons have an electronic contact that transmits a charge to the priming mixture when the trigger is pulled. Thus, there is no firing pin impression for the firearms examiner to use for identification purposes. There would, however, still be the other traditional markings on the cartridge case. Although high cost makes them unpopular, these weapons are currently in production.

## WHAT'S NEXT?

Future developments in the field of fingerprints and firearms are limited only by human imagination. One possibility that may not be too far into the future is hand-carried fingerprint scanners that would allow an investigator to identify an individual and do an instant check against the fingerprint database while the investigator is at the crime scene. With components getting smaller and smaller and the technology continuing to improve, this does not seem too far fetched.

The same miniaturization and portability can be imagined for bullet and cartridge case identification systems. Another item of firearms analysis equipment that might one day be available is a portable vapor analyzer that could analyze the remnant vapor within gun barrels and cartridge cases to establish time since firing. Such a device would help investigators rapidly determine whether persons being interviewed at shooting scenes were telling the truth regarding the events of the shooting.

A hypothetical pair of tools that could revolutionize criminal identification through fingerprints is a device that could scan a crime scene fingerprint followed by a portable DNA analyzer for the fingerprint residue. A combination of a fingerprint scanner and a retinal or iris scanner could do the same for noncriminal identification.

After 40 years of quiet diligence the fields of forensic firearms and fingerprints have been thrust into the limelight, willingly or unwillingly. Nonstop media attention and numerous television and movie dramas have put forensic science in general into the public eye. The term *forensic* has become a household word and is no longer misconstrued as something associated with debate. Although most forensic scientists do not particularly relish all the current attention, there has been some definite good to come out of it all. Instead of having to adapt industrial equipment to forensic applications, manufacturers have begun to recognize the field and are responding with equipment specifically designed for it. The vast array of forensic scientific equipment available on the market is a reflection of this awakening. Doubtless some of the "dream machines" discussed here are on the horizon.

## BREAKTHROUGH: READING FINGERPRINTS EVEN AFTER THEY ARE GONE

Researchers at Leicester have just announced the development of a fingerprint visualization technique that allows for reading a fingerprint even after the print itself has been removed. This new method promises the possible solution of even decade-old unsolved cases.

Forensic scientists at Leicester University's Forensic Research Center have been working with the Northamptonshire police department in England to develop a new method that enables scientists to "visualize fingerprints" even after the print itself has been removed. The technique is specifically for fingerprints on metal objects such as guns, cartridges, cartridge cases, and knives.

"For the first time we can get prints from people who have handled a cartridge case before it was fired," said Dr. John Bond, honorary fellow at Leicester University and scientific support manager at the Northamptonshire police department. The procedure works by applying an electric charge to a metal object—say, a gun or fired cartridge case—which has been coated with a fine-grain conducting powder, similar to that used in photocopiers. Even if the print has been washed off, it leaves a slight corrosion on the metal, and this attracts the powder when the charge is applied, revealing a residual fingerprint. Even if heat from the discharge of a firearm vaporizes a fingerprint, the residual corrosion can allow it to not only be located but also restored, according to Bond.

As a result of the research, cases dating back decades could be reopened because the underlying print never disappears. Bond believes that only abrasive cleaning in which the outer layer of metal is removed can prevent the technique from working. Dr. Bond and Professor Rob Hillman of the chemistry department at the university now intend to take the research forward via a three-year Ph.D. studentship that will commence next year.

This breakthrough is particularly exciting, given the historically low rate of recovery of even the most limited fingerprint-ridge detail on firearms and fired cartridge cases. It is conceivable that this could have an effect similar to that of DNA technology in solving old crimes where no fingerprints were originally found.

## A NEW APPLICATION OF OLD TECHNIQUES

The rate of recovery of identifiable fingerprints on firearms and fired ammunition components has always been small—single-digit percentages being the norm. Thanks to a new application of old technology, this has changed drastically for the Boston police department's fingerprint lab.

The rate of recovery of identifiable fingerprints on guns and fired cartridge cases has gone from the traditional average of around 5 percent to an astounding 32 percent in just more than a year, according to departmental statistics. This jump appears to be the result of changing the way items are processed for fingerprints. Quite simply, rather than packaging guns, fired cartridge cases, and other metal items and sending them to the crime lab for processing, the crime scene unit has begun processing practically everything of forensic interest in the field.

Portable superglue fuming tanks, fuming tents, and fuming wands form the front line of the new approach to on-scene fingerprint processing. Results suggest that it is the packing and unpacking that is responsible for the low recovery rate of fingerprints, particularly on guns and ammunition. The elimination of a lot of extra handling seems to be the secret to getting greatly improved results.

## ARISING LEGAL CHALLENGES

After nearly 100 years of courtroom acceptance both fingerprint identification and firearms identification have become the subjects of challenges as to admissibility. In order to appreciate the legal basis for these challenges, a little legal history is needed with respect to the admissibility of scientific evidence in a court proceeding. The first Supreme Court decision of significance on this subject was in 1923 in the case *Frye v. United States of America*. This case addressed the admissibility of novel scientific evidence and ruled that such evidence was admissible only when "generally accepted by the relevant scientific community." The intent was to keep so-called junk science out of court proceedings. Immediately a majority of the states adopted the "Frye standard," with a number of states still adhering to it.

In 1993 the Supreme Court heard *Daubert v. Merrell Dow Pharmaceuticals, Inc.* The decision that was handed down established the judge as a "gatekeeper" as to the admissibility of scientific evidence. Like *Frye,* it requires acceptance by a majority of the relevant scientific community but goes on to provide guidelines for establishing acceptability. These include the ability to be tested, have been published and peer-reviewed, have an established error rate, and whether standards exist. A number of states adopted the Daubert standard and adhere to it.

Accordingly, when there is a potential question concerning the admissibility of scientific evidence a Frye or a Daubert challenge may be made, depending on the relevant standard. This results in a hearing in which both sides argue their case for admissibility versus inadmissibility. Based on the arguments presented and the applicable standards, the judge makes a ruling.

In 2001 the Supreme Court of Florida reversed the death sentence given in the third trial of Joseph J. Ramirez for the 1983 murder of a night courier (*Joseph J. Ramirez v. State of Florida*), concluding that the tool mark evidence did not meet the Frye standard. In this case a knife in the defendant's possession had been positively identified as having made the tool marks found in the sternum of the decedent. The defense challenged all three of the convictions on the basis of the tool mark evidence not meeting the Frye standard and was successful each time. The court ruled that there were no criteria for identification that were generally accepted in the field (tool mark examiners).

Similar challenges have been made specifically to firearms identification, but these have been unsuccessful to date. The author participated in a Daubert challenge to firearms identification in which the question of criteria for identification was raised. That occurred in Texas, a Daubert state. The judge in that case ruled in favor of firearms identification meeting the Daubert standard.

In general courts have been hesitant to throw out what has been accepted for so many years. That all changed in 2007 in a murder trial in Baltimore, Maryland, in which fingerprint evidence was the key evidence linking a suspect to the crime. In an unprecedented move in response to a defense motion, the judge ruled that the fingerprint evidence would not be admissible at trial. In one full swoop 100 years of accepted technology was thrown out. The judge cited that the ACE-V (analysis, comparison, evaluation, and verification) method was "subjective" and prone to error. The misidentification of a fingerprint in the Madrid bombing case in 2004 by FBI experts was cited by the judge as supporting the unreliability of the technique. The judge stated that while the ACE-V method may be acceptable under the Daubert standard, there was insufficient supporting documentation to allow it.

The ramifications of the Baltimore case are yet to be determined; only time will likely tell. The responses to Frye and Daubert challenges to both firearms identification and fingerprint identification by the scientific communities had begun long before the Baltimore fingerprint case and the Florida tool mark case. It has been recognized for some time that research into the determination of error rate and the establishment of criteria for identification is needed. Both the firearms community and the fingerprint community have established study groups to work on these issues. As of this writing these are still works in progress. The ability to identify a fingerprint to a specific individual or to identify a bullet to a specific gun is not in question, what is in question is how to define when there is an identification and when there is not. It will be interesting to watch all this unfold. Perhaps the reader will have an opportunity one day to weigh in on the issue.

# GLOSSARY

**action**   the working mechanism for chambering, cocking, firing, and ejecting in a firearm. Examples include falling block, rolling block, lever, and slide.

**AFIS (automated fingerprint identification system)**   a system that electronically compares questioned fingerprints against a database of fingerprints composed mainly of persons who have served in the military or who have been arrested

**ALS (alternate light source)**   a source of light that emits only a certain wavelength of light such that certain components of latent fingerprints will fluorence and be made visible; forensic science light

**amido black**   organic compound that reacts with blood to produce a blue-black color

**angle of impact**   the interior (acute) angle of the axis of the path of a bullet connecting with a target

**annular rim**   in firearms examination, the outer circumference of the cartridge case base (location of primer in rim fire cartridges)

**antimony sulfide**   a component of most primers that acts as a fuel

**ballistics**   the study of projectile motion, often confused with firearms identification

**barium nitrate**   a component of most priming mixtures that acts as an oxidizer

**bird shot**   a general term for any shot smaller than buckshot

**bolt action**   a firearm design in which the breech is always in line with the bore and the weapon is loaded, unloaded, and cocked manually. There are two principal types of bolt action firearms: rotating and straight pull.

**bore**   the interior of a barrel forward of the chamber

**breech block**   a metal block that closes the aperture at the back part of a rifle or gun barrel

**breech face**   the part of the breech block or bolt that is against the base of the cartridge case or shot shell during firing

**broach**   in firearms manufacture, a rifling cutter that cuts all the grooves simultaneously

**buckshot**   lead pellets ranging in diameter from 0.20 inch to 0.36 inch and normally fired in shotguns

**bullet**   the projectile portion of a cartridge

**bullet jacket**   a metallic covering over a bullet core that allows the bullet to feed smoothly through the bore of an automatic or semiautomatic firearm

**caliber**   the cross-sectional diameter of the barrel of a firearm, measured from land to land

**calipers**   a device consisting of two movable jaws or legs used to measure distance, thickness, or width

**carbon powder**   fingerprint powder made from finely divided carbon

**cartridge**   an individual unit of ammunition consisting of a cartridge case, bullet, powder charge (propellant), and primer

**cartridge case**   the container encasing the individual components of a round of ammunition

**center fire**   a cartridge design in which the primer is located at the center of the base (head)

**chamber**   in a firearm, the rear part of the barrel bore that has been machined for a specific cartridge. Revolver cylinders are multichambered.

**chamber marks**   individual characteristics imparted to the chamber walls during machining

**chemical enchancement**   in fingerprinting, the use of any variety of chemical reagents to assist in the visualization of a latent fingerprint through chemical reaction with one of the components of the fingerprint residue

**chemical etchant**   a chemical reagent used to dissolve metals and assist in the restoration of obliterated serial numbers

**choke**   in a shotgun, constriction in the muzzle end of the barrel to reduce scattering of the shot

**class characteristics**   qualities that distinguish a collection of items as members of a discrete group, particularly those caused by the processes that made them

**clip**   *See* MAGAZINE

**cock**   to place a firing mechanism under spring tension

**dactylography**   the study of fingerprints for the purposes of identification

**disk powder**   a form of gunpowder that is extruded (forced through a mold) and cut into small disks

**double action**   a type of firing system in which a single pull of the trigger cocks and releases the hammer

**ejection**   the expulsion of a fired cartridge case or shot shell

**ejector marks**   the marks left on the base (head) of a cartridge case or shot shell by the ejector during the process of ejection

**etch**   to produce a mark on a hand material such as metal by corroding away part of the surface

**fingerprint card**   a paper card divided into sections, one for each finger and one for each palm surface, for collecting ink imprints of a person's fingerprints

**fingerprint residue**   a combination of water, salt, protein compounds, and oils

**firearm**   a small arms weapon, such as a rifle or pistol, from which a projectile is fired by gunpowder

**firing pin**   a plunger in the firing mechanism of a firearm that strikes the cartridge primer and initiates ignition

**firing pin impression**   the impression that a firing pin makes at the base of the cartridge upon impact with the primer

**friction ridge**   the raised areas of the palm surface of the hand and the sole surface of the foot that allows gripping. Friction ridges are the patterns recorded in fingerprinting.

**function testing**   the examination of a firearm for operability and firing capability

**general rifling characteristics**   the number, width, and direction of twist of rifling grooves

**Griess test**   a chemical test for nitrites, used to detect gunpowder residue around bullet holes

**grooves**   in firearms, the helical groove in the interior of a barrel to impart spin on the bullet; rifling

**gunshot residue**   gunpowder and primer residue that a firearm discharges when it is fired

**hammer**   the part of a firearm that by its fall or action causes a firing pin to strike the primer, causing the ignition of the primer

**hammer forging**   the process of forming the interior and exterior of a firearm barrel by hammering

**identification**   the determination that two objects, one a known and the other an unknown, had a common origin based on the presence of individual characteristics

**individual characteristics**   accidental, random marks used to identify tool marks as coming from a particular weapon or tool.

**inkless fingerprinting**   a special fingerprint process that puts a clear substance on the fingers and then transfers the ridge detail to a special paper, producing a visual fingerprint without the use of fingerprint ink

**iris**   the colored area of the eye that surrounds the lens

**land**   in firearms, the raised area between two grooves in the interior of a barrel to impart spin on the bullet; rifling

**latent fingerprint**   a fingerprint that is not visible to the unaided eye

**lead azide**   a chemical compound used in most primers to aid in the ignition process

**leuco crystal violet**   an organic chemical that reacts with blood to produce a violet color; used as a presumptive test for the presence of blood

**lever action**   a type of firearms action that uses a lever to move the breech mechanism

**luminol**   an organic compound that reacts with heme (tiny particples in blood) to produce a blue glow in the absence of light, which visualizes the presence of unseen blood in a crime scene

**magazine**   a device that holds and automatically loads cartridges into the chamber of a firearm

**magna powder**   finely divided iron filings used to enhance latent fingerprints on paper surfaces

**major case prints**   inked fingerprints that include all fingers and the palms of both hands

**micrometer**   a precision measuring device used to measure small distances or thicknesses

**negative impression**   the result of touching a surface with a clean hand or finger and removing surface material; an indentation or disturbance of the surface

**NIBIN (National Integrated Bullet Identification Network)** a system for electronic comparison of bullets and cartridge cases entered into databases across the country

**ninhydrin** an organic compound that reacts with amino acids to produce a purple-colored complex

**nitrocellulose powder** a smokeless propellant whose principal ingredient is nitrocellulose, a low explosive

**nitroglycerin** a high explosive and component of double-based gunpowder

**patent fingerprint** a fingerprint that is visible to the unaided eye

**pellet** a common term for the small, spherical shot used in shot shells

**plastic fingerprint** a fingerprint impressed into a pliable medium, such as putty

**plumb bob** a cone-shaped metal object used to establish a line perpendicular to the earth; the plumb bob is attached to a loose wire or line and suspended with the point of the bob oriented toward the ground

**polygonal rifling** rifling with rounded edges instead of the usual square edges

**positive impression** the result of a transfer of material, such as blood, from the finger onto another surface

**powder stippling** the speckled pattern made by powder particles striking the skin and embedding and/or leaving a burn or bruise

**primer** in firearms, a shock-sensitive explosive mixture that initiates burning of the propellant

**propellant** the powder charge inside a shot shell or cartridge case that provides thrust to the projectile

**retina** the area of the eye behind the cornea, lens, pupil, and iris that contains the optic nerve

**rifling** *See* GROOVES

**rifling characteristics** *See* GENERAL RIFLING CHARACTERISTICS

**slug** a single projectile for a shotgun

**sodium rhodizonate** a chemical test used to determine if lead residues are present on a surface, such as fabric

**soot** carbonaceous material produced by the combustion of gunpowder, resulting in fine black particles

**superglue fuming**   the process of making latent fingerprints visual through contact with fumes of cyanoacrylate ester

**tool mark**   any impression, scratch, gouge, cut, or abrasion made when a tool is brought into contact with another object

**tool mark, impressed**   the mark produced when a tool presses against another surface with enough force to leave an impression

**tool mark, striated**   a mark produced with a combination of force and motion

# FURTHER READING

Ashbaugh, David R. *Quantitative/Qualitative Friction Ridge Analysis: An Introduction to Basic and Advanced Ridgeology.* London: CRC Press, 1999. This text gives the reader a basic introduction to fingerprint identification principles as well as discussing advanced techniques.

Association of Firearm and Tool Mark Examiners Web site. Available online. URL: http://www.afte.org. Accessed December 27, 2007. At this Web site members of the firearms community and the general public may access firearms-related information.

Beaver, Colin. *Fingerprints: The Origin of Crime Detection and the Murder Case That Launched Forensic Science.* New York: Hyperion Books, 2002. This text uses a landmark case to discuss the origin of modern crime detection and fingerprint identification.

Chisum, W. Jerry, and Brent E. Turvey. *Crime Reconstruction.* San Diego, Calif.: Academic Press, 2007. This text gives the reader an insight into the history, philosophy, and methodology of crime reconstruction of all types.

Cole, Simon A. "More Than Zero: Accounting for Error in Latent Fingerprint Identification." *Journal of Criminal Law and Criminology* 95 (2005): 985–1,078. This article offers the reader extensive insight into the problems associated with assessment of the rate of error in fingerprint identification.

Cowger, J. F. *Friction Ridge Skin: Comparison and Identification of Fingerprints.* Boca Raton, Fla.: CRC Press, 1993. This text covers the principles of modern fingerprint identification.

DiMaio, V. J. M., and D. DiMaio. *Gunshot Wounds: Practical Aspects of Firearms, Ballistics, and Forensic Techniques.* 2d ed. Boca Raton, Fla.: CRC Press, 1999. This text focuses on the pathological aspects associated with modern firearms identification.

Eckert, William G. *Introduction to Forensic Sciences.* 2d ed. Boca Raton, Fla.: CRC Press, 1997. The chapters on both fingerprints and firearms provide the reader with additional information.

FirearmsID.com: An Introduction to Forensic Firearms Identification Web Site. Available online. URL: http://www.firearmsid.com. Accessed December 30, 2007. This is a site that contains extensive basic firearms information that may be accessed by the general public. It is particularly suitable for students

German, Ed. "Problem Idents: Errors vs. Idents." Available online. URL: http://onin.com/fp/problemidents.html. Accessed January 2, 2008. This Web site is devoted to fingerprint misidentifications and problem identifications, particularly the infamous FBI misidentification of the fingerprint in the Madrid bombing of March 11, 2004.

Gilbert, James G. *Criminal Investigation.* 5th ed. Upper Saddle River, N.J.: Prentice Hall Press, 2001. This text offers additional reading concerning the development of both firearms identification and fingerprint identification.

Haag, Lucien C. *Shooting Incident Reconstruction.* San Diego, Calif.: Academic Press, 2007. This is the second text to be published specifically dealing with the reconstruction of shooting incidents.

Hamby, James E. "Firearms Reference Collections—Their Size, Composition and Use." *Journal of Forensic Sciences* 42 (1997): 461. This article provides insight into the composition of firearms reference collections.

———. "The History of Firearms Identification." *AFTE Journal* 31, no. 3 (1999): 1–27. This article traces the history of firearms identification from its very beginning to the present.

Hatcher, Julian S. *Textbook of Firearms Investigation, Identification, and Evidence.* Plantersville, S.C.: Small-Arms Technical Publishing Co., 1935. This is now a classic. It was the first text ever written on firearms identification.

Hatcher, Julian S., F. J. Jury, and J. Weller. *Firearms Investigation, Identification, and Evidence.* Harrisburg, Pa.: Stackpole Books, 1977. This is an updated version of the first definitive text on firearms identification by Hatcher.

Heard, B. J. *Handbook of Firearms and Ballistics: Examining and Interpreting Forensic Evidence.* West Sussex, UK: John Wiley & Sons, 1997.

This text offers the reader an opportunity to delve into the subject of forensic ballistics.

Hueske, E. E. *Practical Analysis & Reconstruction of Shooting Incidents.* Boca Raton, Fla.: CRC Press, 2006. This is the first text to be published on the philosophy and methodology of shooting incident reconstruction.

Lee, Henry C., and Robert E. Gaensslen. *Advances in Fingerprint Technology.* 2d ed. Boca Raton, Fla.: CRC Press, 2001. This text discusses the advances that have been made in fingerprint technology since the introduction of AFIS and ACE-V.

Lin, C. H., J. H. Liu, J. W. Osterburg, and J. D. Nicol. "Fingerprint Comparison I: Similarity of Fingerprints," *Journal of Forensic Sciences* 27, no. 2 (1982): 290–304. This article discusses the similarities that exist in fingerprints from different persons, including family members.

Mathews, J. H. *Firearms Identification.* 3 vols. Springfield, Ill.: Charles C. Thomas, 1962. This is considered to be the definitive work on firearms identification and continues to be of value to both trainees and experienced firearms examiners.

McMenamin, Jennifer. "Fingerprints Not Reliable—Judge Rules." *Baltimore Sun.* Available online. URL: http://www.baltimoresun.com/news/local/baltimore_county/bal-te.md.co.prints23oct23,0,6370011.story?coll=bal-news-columnists. Accessed December 31, 2007. This article covers a landmark case from 2007 in which a judge ruled that fingerprint identification does not meet the Frye standard for admissibility.

Metropolitan Police. "One Hundred Years of Fingerprints." Available online. URL: http://www.met.police.uk/so/100years. Accessed December 30, 2007. This Web site is devoted to the history of fingerprint identification. It may be accessed by anyone.

Moenssens, Andre A. *Fingerprint Techniques.* Toronto, Canada: Chilton Book Co., 1971. This is considered to be one of the best basic texts ever written on fingerprint identification techniques.

National Institute of Forensic Science, Australia. "Forensic Fact File—Fingerprints." Available online. URL: http://www.nifs.com.au/home.html. Accessed December 30, 2007. This site contains fingerprint identification information that may be accessed by anyone.

Ogle, Robert R., Jr. *Crime Scene Investigation Reconstruction.* Upper Saddle River, N.J.: Pearson/Prentice Hall Press, 2004. This text provides the reader with insight into the reconstruction of crimes involving fingerprints and firearms.

Ridges and Furrows Web site. Available online. URL: http://www. ridgesandfurrows.homestead.com. Accessed December 30, 2007. At this Web site fingerprint examiners and the general public may access information relating to the field of fingerprint examination.

Saferstein, Richard. *Criminalistics: An Introduction to Forensic Science.* Upper Saddle River, N.J.: Pearson/Prentice Hall Press, 2007. This text contains chapters on fingerprints and firearms that provide useful additional information on these disciplines.

Swanson, Charles R., N. C. Chamelin, Robert Taylor, and Leonard Territo. *Criminal Investigation.* 9th ed. New York: McGraw Hill, 2006. This text contains additional information on the development and state of the art of both fingerprint identification and firearms identification.

# INDEX

water, as element of fingerprint 34
water trap 60, 74
weapon. *See* firearm
weapons caches 81
West, Will 45
Whitworth rifles 30
whorl *46, 47,* 83

wipe marks 119
Wooden, William 60
wound ballistics 9, 54

## Z

zero-base protractor 63–64, *65*